God, Where's My Hope?

The Cancer Patient's Book of Paul's Trials

TIM H. GUMM

NORTHWESTERN PUBLISHING HOUSE
Milwaukee, Wisconsin

God, Where's My Hope?

The Cancer Patient's Book of Paul's Trials

TIM H. GUMM

Cover: Cover image used under license from iStock.com
Interior Layout: Mary Jaracz

Northwestern Publishing House
N16W23379 Stone Ridge Dr., Waukesha WI 53188-1108
www.nph.net
© 2024 by Northwestern Publishing House
Published 2024
Printed in the United States of America
ISBN 978-0-8100-2948-4
ISBN 978-0-8100-2949-1 (e-book)

24 25 26 27 28 29 30 31 32 33   10 9 8 7 6 5 4 3 2 1

To Linda, who shares my hope

FOREWORD

Share the story! Make it real and human. We are familiar with the principle. Reporters go to the site of breaking news and look for a witness to tell the story. They put a microphone in front of someone who has seen what happened. The words from someone who has been there and witnessed compel the story.

That principle stands behind this series of books entitled When Cancer Comes. We wanted to tell the story of cancer patients who struggled with their faith when the voice of Jesus seemed to evaporate in the heat of suffering. How did they find strength and comfort when cancer, like a hot coal, sizzled comfort away? We looked for writers who could tell their stories so that others could grow and find strength. We wanted their stories to be real and human.

Each author settled on a specific section of Scripture to help structure the story and message. One focused on Job, another on Paul, and another on Jeremiah. Each of these biblical characters had a special point to make while enduring pain and misery. Job wondered why God sent him so much suffering. Paul endured much but found a reason even to boast in his suffering. Jeremiah complained about his suffering and the suffering he saw around him.

These trials are not uncommon for cancer patients, so we asked the authors to tell their stories. They have been in the doctors' offices to hear the word *cancer*. They either have experienced the chemotherapy and weaknesses or have seen a loved one struggle with them. They matched their personal stories to these biblical characters and found ways to coax faith and courage to grow.

In the soil of their dark days, God's promises nurtured the flower of faith.

Our prayer is that their stories help you water the flower of your faith using God's promises when your faith droops under each challenge.

John Braun, editor

Contents

In order to keep me from becoming conceited, I was given a thorn in my flesh, a messenger of Satan, to torment me.

2 Corinthians 12:7

Introduction

When life hands you lemons, make lemonade. I've heard that often. There's something to be said for an attitude that looks for and can find good even in the toughest and most difficult situations. Yet the little saying seems wrong when life's trials are so difficult that even the lemons that life hands you are rotten. It's pretty hard to make lemonade. Who would want to?

The apostle Paul had a similar philosophy for tough and challenging times. His attitude was not just a stiff upper lip approach or an "every cloud has a silver lining" hope for a brighter tomorrow while suffering. Paul's philosophy was not based on optimistic wishful thinking. It was based on reality, on fact, on truth.

Cancer is one of those tough and difficult situations. Perhaps you have faced the cancer diagnosis. Perhaps a friend or loved one was diagnosed. So now you may be experiencing a deep sense of loss or impending loss. Cancer, as it does, may be demanding more from you than you think you can possibly give. That's where Paul's trials and struggles offer some important lessons. Although frequently fragile and frail, Paul discovered, "When I am weak, then I am strong." In fact, he boasted about his weaknesses: that the weaker he became, the stronger he was.

> Cancer, as it does, may be demanding more from you than you think you can possibly give.

No, it's not a riddle. It's truth. It's real. It's for you and all of us.

Read on. May you be blessed.

Chapter 1
FIRST BOAST

There are secret things of the heart—secret feelings of inadequacy, secret shame, secret pain, secret doubts, secret fears. We don't share them even with our spouse sometimes. Even in marriage, there's a veneer that covers what we do not wish to share. I understand. My wife, Linda, and I both rode silently to the hospital for the hour-and-a-half drive. It was unusually quiet because our hearts were heavy, thinking the worst. The unknown ahead was a heavy weight that squeezed words from our voices in spite of our deep love for each other.

A year and a half earlier Linda had been diagnosed with chronic lymphocytic leukemia. It's simply referred to as CLL—an easy roll off the tongue. Linda is far from a hypochondriac—closer to someone with a gushing head wound who insists that a bandage will take care of it. But after a rather frightening fainting spell on a flight from Denver to Chicago, she agreed to have things checked out. Blood work led to the diagnosis of CLL.

CLL is a chronic and lifelong disease that can remain somewhat fixed and stable for many years—a person can live a good, long life with it. Linda quickly learned that the disease can also have its way with you. It attacked her immune system. There were frequent infections, resultant infusions, and then a period of wait and see. More blood work. Always more blood work. But then, thankfully, relief. The disease had stabilized. We could breathe. We were on top of it. Life could go on.

Cancer patients and those who love them know that good news might only be temporary. All too soon bad news interrupts the relief. When it comes on the heels of good news, it's all the more devastating. I guess that's all of life, really—those sudden plunges through a trapdoor that take you unexpectedly and surprisingly from the mountaintop to the pit.

> "The LORD is my light and my salvation—whom shall I fear? The LORD is the stronghold of my life—of whom shall I be afraid?" (Psalm 27:1).

Linda and I plunged unexpectedly. We felt on top of things, moving on with life, . . . and then one day her gynecologist revealed the bad news. She had uterine cancer. It was bewildering. Was this new cancer brought on by the CLL? No, the two were unrelated. Did this new cancer mean that the CLL was getting worse? Not necessarily; it's an entirely different deadly thing. Might the CLL be getting worse? The doctor said to take one step at a time: "Let's worry about that after we take care of this."

And so very early one morning, we drove an hour and a half to the hospital. Surgery was scheduled for that morning. It was a quiet drive. I don't know what filled Linda's heart—whatever thoughts filled her heart were kept inside. They weren't to be shared, not even with her lover. Was there anxiety? Was there uncertainty? Was there fear? (Yes, fear—something that Christians aren't supposed to feel and that leads them to wonder if they're even Christians anymore.) Was there utter helplessness in the face of the possible outcome? Was there dread of how the changes might affect our marriage and family?

After Linda was prepped for surgery—robed in a hospital gown and an IV in her arm—she asked me to talk. Not my own words. Not now. She had, in fact, prepared my script, writing it on an index card days earlier. I pulled the card from my shirt pocket, took her hand, and read my lines: "The LORD is my light and my salvation—whom shall I fear? The LORD is the stronghold of my life—of whom shall I be afraid?" (Psalm 27:1).

That's all she wanted to hear. Not me, but the Lord. He was the answer—the one before whom all anxiety, fear, helplessness, weakness, and even death take flight. In him, the weak find, receive, and can actually boast over a core of calm and a peace that passes understanding. Yes, all of this is from him . . . trumping the weakness of the weak.

Now someone might scoff at such a boast and ask, "Is this the same one who was poor and homeless, the same one who history tells us was brutally beaten and crucified under a Roman governor named Pontius Pilate, who died the excruciating death of the cross and then was buried in a borrowed tomb?" Then there's a second question: "Why do you believe he can help?"

Let's be clear: Yes, this is the one, the very same. This is the weak one my weak wife wanted to hear about again, the weak one in whom and from whom my weak wife sought strength. And in him she found it . . . and so much more. If you have questions, come with us on our journey. We believe that Christ died, but he also rose. He was so much more than just a poor, homeless wanderer. He rose from the dead and has the power to help us in every trial.

The apostle Paul had the same faith in Christ. You most likely heard of Paul and may even be quite familiar with him. His story stretches from the scoffer of Christian faith, even becoming an enemy of Christians, to the confessor of a bold, confident faith in the face of many trials. Linda and I found strength, comfort, courage, and reassurance from him. He faced trials as we did and as we all must.

Aside from Jesus Christ, Paul is the central figure on the pages of the New Testament. The book of Acts records Paul's miraculous conversion to Christianity. That was, in fact, not only miraculous but also, humanly speaking, astounding and dumbfounding. Paul at first hated Christ and all who followed him. Born and bred a Jew, Paul was deeply offended by the claim that the carpenter's son from Nazareth was the Jewish Messiah. He was further offended by the claim that this weak one who had been so humiliated and had died at the hands of the Romans on a horrifying cross was in fact the God of heaven—*his* God!—and the only one in whom a person can find salvation. Infuriated and deeply insulted, Paul set out to persecute the followers of Christ, put an end to the Christian movement, and erase the Nazarene's name from the pages of history.

God had other plans. One day, against all human odds, Paul became a Christian himself. Nobody saw it coming, not even Paul, but suddenly this man knew and believed what was truth: that the weak, humble, humiliated, and crucified Jesus of Nazareth was indeed the Lord and Savior of the world. It's all there in Acts chapter 9. It is a testimony not only to God's power to change even an enemy but also to God's amazing, undeserved grace for all humans struggling with life's challenges.

Paul's life took a 180: unbelief to saving faith, darkness to light, death to life. But there was more. The Lord then called Paul to teach, preach, and proclaim Jesus—yes, this weak Jesus—as the world's Lord and Savior. And Paul, compelled by Jesus' saving love, did exactly that. He traveled throughout the Mediterranean world—often retracing his steps; often suffering ridicule and violence, hardship and trouble; often exhausted and utterly weak—to proclaim a weak Christ.

Paul's second mission journey took him to Corinth. At the time, it was one of the leading cities in Greece. It boasted great architecture. It was a commercial center between Rome and the East. Therefore, it enjoyed great wealth, and with that, a variety of philosophies gave the city choices to consider. The pursuit of wisdom and the debate of old and new philosophies, including those about things spiritual and eternal, had become objects of worship in Corinth. Next to wealth, the pursuit of wisdom was a significant goal in life. The Corinthians enjoyed a good back-and-forth between trained orators to get the juices flowing. Point, counterpoint, point, counterpoint, checkmate! It was worth money to hear the eloquent words of the scholars and the skill with which they used them. And the Corinthians paid.

When Paul arrived on the scene, he could have blended in nicely with the culture of those who sought wisdom. He grew up in Tarsus and was a Roman citizen. Paul was highly intelligent, a learned man. He had been instructed in Jerusalem at the feet of the respected Rabbi Gamaliel, one of the best, and became a Pharisee. Paul could have easily held his own in any debate. But his message was not a new brand of human wisdom or philosophy. Instead, he proclaimed the message of God's love in sending Jesus into this world and the promise of eternal life through the suffering and death of Jesus.

Paul showed up with a brand of wisdom that by Corinthian standards—as well as human standards today—was embarrassingly weak and inferior to the deep thoughts of the city's scholars and philosophers. His message was considered foolish, silly, and absurd in this culture that prized and worshiped human intellect and wisdom. Paul's message, by his own admission and in truth, was empty of such wisdom. Paul knew that his message was powerful and able to make those who heard it wise unto salvation. There was no superior eloquence of which to speak. No new and intriguing philosophy was being offered. Rather, Paul's message was simple, clear, and straightforward. And he boasted in this. He had arrived in Corinth not with more human wisdom but with the wisdom of the true God himself. Paul had come proclaiming the good news of Christ, the Son of God, and he stayed in Corinth a year and a half proclaiming that message.

> The one who gave life to all things and powerfully sustains all things to this day—this God became fully human.

For many, the gospel is too much to believe. It is, after all, the story of God himself becoming human. The eternal and timeless Creator who formed the universe by his unlimited and immeasurable power humbled himself to come to earth. Yes, the one who gave life to all things and powerfully sustains all things to this day—this God became fully human. He is subject to no one and no power. He needs nothing and no one, but he came to walk, talk, and breathe like all of us.

Now if God's arrival on the planet had been grand and glorious, some people might more readily accept the story. But that wasn't the case. He arrived unseen, microscopic: an embryo miraculously implanted by the Holy Spirit into the womb of a virgin and confined there for nine months. And already you sense the foolishness. Yes, conception in a virgin's womb, but more: How can the limitless God, whom the universe cannot possibly contain, be limited to a womb? And why? Yes, why would the sovereign God be entirely dependent on his mother?

Now all of this is enough to insult anyone's intelligence. A God so weak and pathetic is certainly no God. But to answer why, we must look at the rest of his life. Jesus stepped into the public eye as a traveling teacher. He gathered a dozen special disciples who would accompany him and learn from him. Those twelve were not wealthy donors or influential, powerful backers. They could not protect him from those who wanted to destroy him. They fled into the night when Jesus was arrested by his enemies. Jesus was bound. His disciples immediately disowned him and denied their association with him. The religious leaders condemned him to death and then led him to the Roman governor to carry out an execution based on lies and fabrications. Jesus was beaten mercilessly. A scourge was used to rip the flesh from his back. A crown of thorns was woven and pressed into his scalp to ridicule his claims of kingship. His deeply bruised and swollen face was covered with spittle. Portions of his beard were torn out. And then at a place called Calvary outside of Jerusalem's city wall, Jesus was stripped of his clothing and nailed to the beams of a Roman cross to suffer the shame of hanging naked before God and the world and to undergo the bloody horror and hell that is death by crucifixion.

The question *why* becomes even more important. Has anyone ever known a weakness like this? A humiliation more degrading? It is no wonder that so many will feel that their intelligence is being insulted when they're told that Jesus of Nazareth is the almighty God of the universe. To them this message is just so much foolishness!

And yet this is true: Jesus is the weak one of whom my weak wife wanted to hear before she was taken into surgery—the weak one in whom she found a strength in which to boast. You see, Linda agreed with what the apostle Paul wrote in a letter to the church in Corinth. The city oozed human wisdom and prided itself on a human wisdom that logically dismissed Christ as foolishness, but Paul wrote, "The foolishness of God is wiser than human wisdom, and the weakness of God is stronger than human strength" (1 Corinthians 1:25).

> Jesus is the weak one of whom my weak wife wanted to hear before she was taken into surgery—the weak one in whom she found a strength in which to boast.

In the face of cancer there may be help in medical science to give us relief and health. We see that. But even if we become cancer free, we have not overcome an obstacle beyond the help of medical science. All of us will die. That's a fact that is 100 percent accurate—no exceptions. Philosophies and human wisdom all seek a solution, but whatever the solution imagined and discussed, it is just so much theory. Even if one denies the life after death, we will all have to stand before the Lord of all when we leave this life. What could you possibly offer God that would move him to give you eternal life? Nothing you have. Nothing you do. Nothing you think. Nothing in your life is enough.

The Son of God took upon himself the guilt and sin of the entire world and then, in utter weakness, offered up his own life as the full and final payment for that guilt and sin. There was no other way. Corinthian wisdom and that of our world today think this is foolishness, but no human can earn a place into God's heart or appease his divine justice. No combination of decent living, paying, praying, or good and kindly works will do. It's not enough; it's not enough to pay for sin, not when the holy God of the Bible solemnly declares that there is no other payment and punishment for our sin but the death of hell.

Only God himself can rescue us. And he did. He loved the world so much that he gave his Son for us. Jesus freely made himself nothing for us so that on the cross of Calvary he might make the full payment for our sin in our place: dying our death, enduring our hell, appeasing divine justice, and securing the forgiveness of our sins. Yes, through this Christ—through God himself making himself so weak—comes our salvation! We may stand before the Almighty at death because Jesus has done what we could not do. No wonder Paul boasted in a weak Christ and his *foolish* message about Christ. Christ Jesus is the Lord and Savior, and by his chosen and love-born weakness, he gained our eternal glory. Because of that love, both Linda and I trust him for our forgiveness and the hope he came to give all the world—to you too.

> Linda and I trust him for our forgiveness and the hope he came to give all the world—to you too.

What Paul had come to know and believe and what every child of God knows and believes is that the utter weakness of Christ is actually his greatest strength of all. It is the power of his love to save the world and, in the power of his love to save, to *do* these things: willingly humble himself, voluntarily set aside the glory that is his from eternity—to be restricted and held tightly in a young virgin's womb, born in a stable, and placed in a manger. This is power! It is the power to allow the humiliation, to permit the arrest, to submit to the beatings and abuse, to suffer the ridicule without retaliation, to remain silent to the blasphemous things that filled his ears, and then to willingly endure the torture and death of Calvary's cross.

Now another question comes to mind. It's not only "Why did Jesus endure such humiliation?" but also "Why do Christians find strength in him and understand that he is Lord of all? Why do they turn to him in the darkest days and the greatest weaknesses?" Jesus' love for all humanity is the reason why he willingly laid down his life. He loved us deeply enough to sacrifice himself for us. His plan from the beginning was to give us eternal life. His message is not just some intelligent human speculation. He actually demonstrated that he had the solution to death. He rose from the dead. He is the one who has the answer, the wisdom, and the power. He is the one we want to listen to and rely on. No one else has ever made the claim to have overcome death.

Here's powerful news: Jesus overcame death. He loved us and still loves us each day in each and every trial or success. Paul learned that important truth, proclaimed it, lived it, and wrote about it. He wrote, "He who did not spare his own Son, but gave him up for us all—how will he not also, along with him, graciously give us all things?" (Romans 8:32). Here's the answer to the second question.

> Here's powerful news: Jesus overcame death.

Christians find strength in Jesus because of his love—a love that continues to care for those who love him.

But this truth enters into real life. Like my wife, maybe you have learned that the disease can have its way with you. You go where cancer tells you to go and spend your time as cancer tells you to spend it. You submit, without a say, to the fatigue, nausea, treatments, or surgery—a victim of sorts. And you deal alone with the worries and anguish in your heart that you don't share: the fear, the uncertainty, the sense of absolute helplessness and weakness before cancer. These are very personal things, aren't they? And even when good news comes—a favorable test result, a shrinking tumor, a successful operation, a little more vigor than usual, a good day for a change—even then you've learned to receive it tentatively, cautiously, without a whole lot of bragging. There may be that trapdoor waiting to open and swallow you again.

That doesn't mean you can't find anything in your weakness to boast about. Paul, extremely weak himself, will help you discover these things in the chapters that follow. But for now, let me urge you to make Christ your very first boast. That was Paul: before he boasted in his own weakness, he boasted in his weak Christ. Do the same. God loves you deeply and dearly, even you with cancer. There is nothing you can do to diminish that love and nothing you can do to add to it. Christ became weak for you. It's done. He lived a life of perfection and gave you the credit for it. So boast. He died humble and humiliated on the cross of Calvary. Every sin and offense in your life that should separate you from the Almighty forever has been covered by Jesus' blood and forgiven. It is finished. And now risen from the grave, Christ assures you that, through him, you are God's own child. He produces a wonderful core of calm and tranquility by promising that you are at peace with God regardless of life's circumstances. It is so. He made it possible for you to live every moment now in the certain hope of unending life in heaven. Not just a wish. Not just a dream. But a joyful expectation of an eternity without weakness or pain—an eternity of glory that will most certainly happen because of Jesus Christ, who became so weak for all of us. Whatever cancer is doing to you today, no matter where it is taking you, make this your boast.

> He made it possible for you to live every moment now in the certain hope of unending life in heaven.

May I suggest, then, a hidden blessing behind the weakness and frailty that your disease may bring, one you may not have considered? Might your weakness be giving you an opportunity—a rather special opportunity that others aren't given—to remember and reflect on your weak Jesus and what his weakness means for you and so to boast again and again?

Consider Paul. His proclaiming of Christ the Savior in Corinth had, by God's power, brought many to faith in Christ the Savior. That's what Paul did in his ministry all over the Mediterranean world. He had suffered much as he proclaimed the gospel. He had been flogged, experienced shipwreck, kept in prison, and suffered hunger and thirst. Why did he endure all these trials? Because he knew Jesus loved him, had suffered in weakness and humility for him and the people he met, and because he was confident of not only God's promises of eternal life but also God's care for him in his pain and struggle.

Paul acknowledged and rightly linked his own weakness and humility with those of Christ. Paul wrote, "For to be sure, he was crucified in weakness, yet he lives by God's power. Likewise, we are weak in him, yet by God's power we will live with him in our dealing with you" (2 Corinthians 13:4). For Paul (and this should have been the case for the Corinthians as well), weakness was the indisputable validation that his ministry and the gospel he proclaimed were of God. At the same time, Paul allowed his own weakness to serve as a reminder of his Savior's weakness—a chosen weakness that, for Christ, was actually a path to eternal glory, not only for himself but for Paul as well. And Paul boasted of his weaknesses, "Therefore I will boast all the more gladly about my weaknesses, so that Christ's power may rest on me. . . . For when I am weak, then I am strong" (2 Corinthians 12:9,10).

Will you allow your weakness to serve the same good purpose: a blessed reminder of Christ? Perhaps cancer is confining you somehow. Remember that Jesus too was confined, willingly confined to a womb . . . for you. Perhaps cancer is leaving you fatigued beyond anything you thought possible. Jesus too gave himself up to fatigue, stumbling under the weight of his cross . . . for you. Perhaps cancer is asking more from you than you think you can possibly give. Jesus too was asked to give, and driven by his love for you, he gave the ultimate—he gave himself to the death and hell of the cross. All of this for you, weak one. All of this to give you peace and pardon. All of this to give you hope and a certain future. All of this to give you strength and life. Yes, all of this weakness to give you glory that will never end. That's a Savior in whom you can take pride. That's a Savior about whom you can boast.

And so I took Linda's hand and read, "The LORD is my light and my salvation—whom shall I fear? The LORD is the stronghold of my life—of whom shall I be afraid?" (Psalm 27:1).

Now boast, weak one. Boast in Jesus.

Chapter 2
HANGING ON

At one time, media mogul Ted Turner was one of the wealthiest and most powerful men in America. He is probably best known as a philanthropist, the onetime owner of the Atlanta Braves franchise, and the founder of Cable News Network (CNN), the first 24-hour cable news channel. At one time Ted Turner was also known as a Christian but no longer.

In an April 23, 2001, article for *The New Yorker* entitled "The Lost Tycoon," writer and journalist Ken Auletta mentioned the reason for Ted Turner's fall from the Christian faith.

> By the time he was a teen-ager, Ted knew that he did not want to join his father's business. He was religious, and he decided that he was going to be a missionary. Then his sister became ill. He was fifteen when Mary Jane, who was twelve, contracted systemic lupus erythematosus, a disease in which the immune system attacks the body's tissue. She was racked with pain and constantly vomiting, and her screams filled the house. Ted regularly came home and held her hand, trying to comfort her. He prayed for her recovery; she prayed to die. After years of misery, she succumbed. Ted lost his faith. "I was taught that God was love and God was powerful," he says, "and I couldn't understand how someone so innocent should be made or allowed to suffer so."

Ted Turner was neither the first nor the last to abandon his faith and turn from God because of adversity. In fact, Jesus himself spoke frankly about this very thing: that hardship and trouble may lead a child of God to walk away from God. He once told a parable about a farmer who went into his field to sow seed (Matthew chapter 13). The seed, Jesus explained, is the Bible's good message about Christ the Savior that produces faith and brings a person into God's eternal kingdom. But it's not unusual, Jesus continued, that faith, when allowed to remain weak, may very well succumb to "trouble or persecution" or "the worries of this life and the deceitfulness of wealth" (Matthew 13:21,22). And because these troubles, challenges, and difficulties are the reality of everyday life, faith in the Savior is, in truth, always under attack. It is an inescapable part of living as sinful people in a sin-spoiled and fallen world.

> Cancer is one of those troubles and worries of this life. It can very often be a special and formidable challenge to one's faith in Christ.

Are you feeling that right now? Are you feeling the attack? Cancer is one of those troubles and worries of this life. It can very often be a special and formidable challenge to one's faith in Christ and one's relationship with God. It can, as you may know, lead a person to doubt God's power and goodness. Like Ted Turner, many defiantly question God and his ways, "If God loves me so, why would he let this happen?" The pull to abandon him is real.

Yet here you are: dealing with cancer . . . and hanging on. Hanging on to the one who became so weak for you because his love for you is so strong. Hanging on to your forgiveness, your peace, your certain hope, your joy, your life with no end, your Savior Jesus Christ. Hanging on to your boast in the blessings Jesus gives you. And this doesn't mean that your faith in him isn't taking a beating. The fact that you're hanging on doesn't mean, necessarily, that you have no questions or doubts or that you're not puzzled or profoundly tested by his dealings with you. Nonetheless, you're still hanging on. Where other intelligent and reasonable people might have turned and run from him, you're still committed, still dedicated to the One who is your life.

And now are you looking for something in which you can continue to boast in your time of weakness? This is it, and it's not a trivial thing. Boast in your dedication and commitment to Christ—in the fact that you're not letting go of him even in the worst of circumstances. True, you may feel uncomfortable in boasting; it always leaves a somewhat unpleasant odor behind. But do it nonetheless: Boast in Christ and the power he has given you to hang on. You won't be alone in doing so. The apostle Paul was a boaster too.

> Boast in Christ and the power he has given you to hang on.

Paul boasted in Christ. After he left the Corinthians, the congregation was troubled by false teachers who claimed to be anything but weak. These self-appointed preachers had come with a different gospel and were proclaiming a different Christ—a gospel and a Christ that were much more in tune with the human philosophies that colored the landscape and culture. What is more, these trained orators and gifted speakers did not hesitate to compare themselves with their absent predecessor, boasting of their superior abilities, their more impressive credentials, and their deeper dedication to ministry. They were boasting of themselves, undermining Paul's work and ministry, and drawing the Corinthian Christians away from the foolish and apparent weakness of the gospel. These false teachers were claiming that the Corinthians needed more, and they gathered a following for themselves. Without discernment and with so little resistance, the sheep in Corinth followed the false shepherds.

Paul was deeply distressed when he learned of the situation and deeply concerned not just for his office as a true and called apostle of Christ but more so for the honor and glory of Christ himself and the souls of the Corinthians who were now forsaking Christ. It was for these reasons that Paul was compelled to defend himself and his ministry even if it meant a little boasting of his own. Now, boasting was repulsive and loathsome to Paul; he was extremely uncomfortable, uneasy, and embarrassed in doing so. He wrote that when he boasted of his accomplishments and knowledge, he was "speaking as a fool" (2 Corinthians 11:21). But for the sake of those souls in the Corinthian congregation who were being lured and led away from Christ the Savior, Paul was convinced that it was completely necessary to counter the boasting of the super-apostles with his own.

In 2 Corinthians chapter 11, the apostle begins by addressing certain charges that had been hurled against him—charges that, although absurd and without foundation, had nonetheless twisted the Corinthians' opinion of Paul, his ministry, and Christ. The false teachers accused Paul of refusing to accept pay from them. All the other teachers in Corinth were not bashful about accepting money. Paul countered that he did not accept remuneration because he did not want to give even the slightest impression that the gospel, like the human philosophies of the day, had a fee attached to it. Paul had come to Corinth to give freely the truth of God's free gift of salvation through Christ Jesus alone.

Paul also *foolishly* boasted of the hard work he had done for Christ, the suffering he endured, often going without food, even his escape from Damascus when he was threatened with arrest. He wrote, "The God and Father of the Lord Jesus, who is to be praised forever, knows that I am not lying. In Damascus the governor under King Aretas had the city of the Damascenes guarded in order to arrest me. But I was lowered in a basket from a window in the wall and slipped through his hands" (2 Corinthians 11:31-33). Think about it. To suffer such humiliation, embarrassment, rejection, and weakness—having to sneak and slither out of the city in such an inglorious way—might finally lead one to say, "This isn't worth it. I didn't sign up for this."

If these false teachers were bashing Paul, they had nothing on him—nothing at all. His boasts about his own accomplishments were nothing, even though his dedication was deeper, his commitment was stronger, and his spirit of sacrifice was greater. Instead, he boasted of his weakness—a thorn in the flesh—that tormented him even after he had prayed three times for the Lord to take it away. His pain and torment drove him to rely on Christ. He wrote, "I will boast all the more gladly about my weaknesses, so that Christ's power may rest on me" (2 Corinthians 12:9). In spite of severe sufferings and trials in his ministry that would have led others to give up, Paul would not let go. He hung on to Christ. Yes, Paul hung on. He would not let go.

Someone might look at you today and wonder why you are hanging on to a crucified Savior who humbled himself and suffered. Please don't make light of it. Please don't make light of what you're dealing with and how you're hanging

> Someone might look at you today and wonder why you are hanging on to a crucified Savior who humbled himself and suffered.

on. And please know that those with you are doing the same: hanging on. A deadly disease can very well cut a life short and shatter so many dreams. But hang on to that Savior. Fear and uncertainty and anger and bewilderment and so many emotions previously unknown overwhelm you. But hang on. There may be more: surgery and hair-removing chemo and pain and more surgery and nausea-producing radiation and weakness and fear and fatigue-filled days and sleepless nights and more surgery. But hang on. Somehow hang on to him. And there's the loss of what makes a woman feel attractive and feminine or what makes a man feel attractive and masculine and the burden of concern over the people in one's life who might have to move on alone. But hang on. And then you count the exorbitant expense of the whole thing, the doctors and surgeons. Finally, if healed, you may worry that the whole thing might start again with a reoccurrence of the disease. But still hang on to Jesus. That weak, humble, and crucified Lord did not stay dead. He rose. He has eternal life for you and strength for you to hang on. And if you really think about it, that's an amazing thing.

On so many occasions during the years of my marriage, I have walked in on Linda as she was reading the Bible or praying. It's not infrequent that this daughter of the Lord will do what all of God's children do: speak and listen to their Father. What has struck me is that her speaking and listening never stopped or seemed to slow after her diagnoses of CLL and uterine cancer. Those trials could have knocked the dedication to the Lord out of anybody. That isn't to say she neither had struggles of faith nor questions about the Lord's dealings with her; I'm sure she did. That doesn't mean she didn't cry or worry or become depressed; I know she did. Yet she wouldn't stop speaking and listening to God. "He is still my Savior. Even now. He is still my Lord. Even now. He is still my first love. Yes, even now," she confessed.

> Those trials could have knocked the dedication to the Lord out of anybody.

Again, if you really think about it, it's an amazing thing, isn't it? This faith, this trust, this commitment to Christ in spite of severe trials. Sure, it's being tested, beaten, and battered and may ebb and flow, but it's still there. Amazing! And it is truly something in which to boast: "I'm still committed. I'm still hanging on to him. Still." Christ's power comes from the promises he made.

But how do you explain it? Because it's unreasonable—this hanging on when any sensible and intelligent person would understand that it's time to let go. How do you explain it?

Listen again to Paul. Listen carefully. As he continued his reluctant boasting, he explained his own unreasonable commitment to the Lord. Yet his explanation reveals that all of his boasting was actually a boast in the Lord. "I must go on boasting. Although there is nothing to be gained, I will go on to visions and revelations from the Lord. I know a man in Christ . . ." The man was Paul; yet Paul, so uneasy with boasting, speaks of himself in the third person. "I know a man in Christ who fourteen years ago was caught up to the third heaven. Whether it was in the body or out of the body I do not know—God knows.

And I know that this man—whether in the body or apart from the body I do not know, but God knows—was caught up to paradise and heard inexpressible things, things that no one is permitted to tell" (2 Corinthians 12:1-4).

Years before Paul suffered the hardships and weaknesses connected with his ministry, the Lord Jesus had given him a remarkable gift: a vision, a peek at the glory of heaven that was awaiting Paul and all believers in Christ. What Paul saw and heard in that vision were things so glorious and thrilling that it's impossible for the human tongue to describe them; they were awesome "inexpressible things" (2 Corinthians 12:4). Yet this Paul would be able to say: his vision from the Lord, this vision of his salvation in Christ alone, this vision of his own unending glory in heaven strengthened him and enabled him to press on and remain deeply committed to the God of his salvation. Even in the face of hardships and weaknesses, Paul did it! He hung on! Tenaciously! And others saw it. And he boasted of it. Yet his boast, you see, was not really in himself—not at all—but in the God who by his power in that gospel vision fortified and enabled Paul to endure, hang on, and never forsake Christ.

> [Paul's boast], you see, was not really in himself—not at all—but in the God who by his power in that gospel vision fortified and enabled Paul to endure, hang on, and never forsake Christ.

So how do you explain it in yourself: your unreasonable commitment to Christ? I assume that you've had no vision from the Lord, no peek from him into the hallways of heaven. So how do you explain it? What has kept you committed to Jesus even in this time of severe hardship and weakness?

The truth is that the Lord Jesus comes to you as he came to Paul, not in a vision, most likely, but where he has promised: in Word and wine and bread and water. He comes personally, intimately, lovingly, gently, yet powerfully on the pages of the Bible and in the sacraments that he's given to his people, saying, "Yes, these too are awe-inspiring and inexpressible things. But listen. Look. Touch. Taste. Here I am—the forgiveness of your sins. It's true. And it's done. Here I am. With you. Your life. Your peace. Your comfort. Your brother and Savior. Your Lord and your God. Here I am. Your certain hope. I rose from death. I give you a certain and unending future. I will be your strength and stamina. Here I am, drawing closer to you and drawing you closer to me."

> Each day he has given you the strength to remain committed to the God who has saved you. It is only by his power—hanging on in spite of your weakness.

And others will sense it. Or perhaps they'll hear it from your lips or see it in your gracious demeanor. Your light is your astonishing and irrational commitment to Christ. And it's an opportunity to boast—to boast in Christ before others—to boast in the fact that, by the miraculous power of his gospel, he has embraced you and empowered you to embrace him. Each day he has given you the strength to remain committed to the God who has saved you. It is only by his power—hanging on in spite of your weakness.

Remember Paul's thorn in the flesh! Paul recognized that not only did this particular weakness magnify God's greatness and strength in his life, but it also led him to treasure God's mercy and love. Paul understood himself—the proud and ugly side found in every human that very well could have turned Paul to think highly of himself because of the vision he had received. Paul wrote, "To keep me from becoming conceited, I was given a thorn in my flesh, a messenger of Satan, to torment me. Three times I pleaded with the Lord to take it away from me" (2 Corinthians 12:7,8).

We can only speculate about the nature of Paul's thorn in the flesh. Some have suggested that his thorn was a chronic and painful cancer. If this was the case, then you know what he was dealing with. You know and can appreciate his repeated prayers for wholeness and strength. And you know and can understand that Paul would see his thorn as a terrible hindrance to his life's work.

God did not remove it. What was God's answer to his prayers? "My grace is sufficient for you, for my power is made perfect in weakness" (2 Corinthians 12:9). Paul had in mind that God would remove his chronic and crippling thorn and restore his strength. God, as is always his way, had something better in mind. God gave Paul an even greater strength than what he had prayed for—the strength of God's saving grace that would enable the apostle not only to cope with his thorn and weakness and hang on to his God but also to see and celebrate the good purpose behind his thorn. As Paul proclaimed the Savior, those who heard and saw him would quickly perceive that there was a greater power behind this weak man; there had to be! It was the power of the Savior Paul was proclaiming.

Realizing all of this, Paul concluded, "Therefore I will boast all the more gladly about my weaknesses, so that Christ's power may rest on me. That is why, for Christ's sake, I delight in weaknesses, in insults, in hardships, in persecutions, in difficulties. For when I am weak, then I am strong" (2 Corinthians 12:9,10). So strong . . . in the Lord.

Now that's a seeming paradox, isn't it? When I'm weak, then I'm strong. Some might say it's an absurdity. But a weak daughter of Christ reads her Bible, listens to her Father, and then speaks to him in prayer. And she boasts. Linda boasts that she belongs to this God. She boasts in his promises to her. Because of those promises, she boasts of his grace and love, hanging on to him and never letting go, even in this terrible time of life. Others may hear her boast. Still others may sense her boast. But, you see, what she is really boasting about is the God of her salvation, who by his speaking and listening to her empowers her to keep listening and speaking to him. And by the truth of his saving love for her that won't and can't let go of her, he empowers her to speak and listen more and more. She can't let go either. She won't.

What kind of God is this?! So loving! Never forsaking! Even, in the darkest moments—in what should be the most hopeless moments—there he is. Real. In his Word. At the font. In the Supper. Personal. Intimate. Just you. Just him. Keeping you close even when cancer is trying to tear you away. Ever committed and dedicated to you and keeping you committed and dedicated to him. Others who have given up may call you a fool. Still others may see it and marvel. You may or may not marvel over it too. Regardless, a God who would do this—who would love you so much to do this for you and in you—is certainly worthy of your boast.

> There he is. . . .
> Keeping you close
> even when cancer
> is trying to tear
> you away.

God has given you a treasure he will not take away. He gives you eternal life, hope for a future beyond the pain and weaknesses. Don't give up on his promises. His gifts are inexpressible and awesome and only he has them for you. As Paul also wrote, "I consider that our present sufferings are not worth comparing with the glory that will be revealed in us" (Roman 8:18).

Go ahead. Hang on.

Chapter 3
WHAT ABOUT ME?

Tantrums are not an uncommon occurrence. Every time I see one, I relive the particular embarrassment that frequently comes with having children. If you're a parent, you know the embarrassment as well.

Picture it. A little child, not quite two years old, is playing with other little ones. The parents have arranged a playdate. It's a delightful scene, even amusing. But then the beauty of it all is suddenly shattered by a single ugly word that comes from one little child's mouth: "Mine!" He repeats it with more force, "*Mine!*" while clutching and hanging on to the book he has snatched. But the book is not his. It belongs to another. Even if it were his, he's too young to make proper use of it. But he insists, and in the opening stage of a tantrum, he screams with a voice that turns heads, "*Mine!*" It all happens so quickly. No warning. Another child joins the possessive tug-of-war. Mom springs from her seat, lifts her flailing child from the developing melee, and then attempts an explanation for the adults, "He's hungry." Other excuses also come to mind, "He hasn't had his nap yet" or "He's just a little cranky today." She wanted to crawl into a hole. I've been there. I've looked for that same hole. I've known the embarrassment. Perhaps you have too.

So often, it seems, *mine* is one of the first words a little child will learn. It may not be the child's very first word, but it usually follows closely on the heels of *mama* and *daddy*. That's revealing. Whether we want to acknowledge it or not, it reveals something rather unappealing about the child: he or she is selfish.

In spite of the training to share, *mine* remains an important word. Now someone may retort, "Well, that's just natural. All little boys and girls are like that." Yes, that's exactly the point: All little boys and girls *are* like that—selfish—and as soon as they're able to express it in a word, they will . . . and do: not *yours* or *ours* but *mine*. Sadly, it isn't a selfishness that will disappear after a nap or a healthy snack. It's not a selfishness that is taught or caught. This ugly side of the little child—the ugly selfishness, self-centeredness, and self-love—*is* just natural. Inherent. Built-in. Hardwired into one's very being so that, from the start, life is about *me*. In other words, from the start, life is all about . . . self. *Me* is my god.

When we grow older, we learn to overcome and hide this *self*-ishness. We realize that it *is* unappealing and unattractive. So we tuck it away. A sense of common decency may allow the guy with only one grocery item to move ahead of us at the check-out line. Common courtesy may lead us to open the door for another or offer to help with packages. Yet it's still there hoping someone will do the same when we need help. Even then we are still naturally built around self. Advertisers picked up on this a long time ago: "You deserve this: perhaps this car, this dress, this refrigerator." We want what we think we deserve. The self within is triggered and answers, "Yes. I guess they're right. I do deserve that."

> Well, cancer, as you undoubtedly have learned, takes you down a road on which you focus quite a bit on you.

So what does all of this have to do with you? Well, cancer, as you undoubtedly have learned, takes you down a road on which you focus quite a bit on you. Perhaps the first thought you had was "Why me?" Like any pressing trouble or hardship in life, cancer may lead you to focus on you; it can easily lead you to a focus on your*self*. At first, you deny the diagnosis. "This must be wrong. I can't have cancer! Not now! There must be some mistake." Soon the denial disappears. Then you feel alone and isolated. How hard it is to tell others! Your spouse or trusted friend may be the exception. But you continue to ask, "Why is this happening to me—to us?" We convince ourselves that even if we would tell others what is weighing heavily on our hearts, they wouldn't care. We're all alone, left to feel sorry for ourselves (because no one else will), to rehash and wallow in our troubles. At times, you may become so wrapped up in you and your disease and what your disease is doing to you that you have little thought for anything or anyone else. The world continues to move on around you and all the other people. Your concern is for *self*. *Self* will always

> Sometimes denial and isolation breed anger and bitterness.

focus on *self*. "Nobody knows my weakness and nobody really cares. People politely asked and wished me well when I was first diagnosed, but that concern has ended; they're back to their lives. But what about me? What about *me*?"

Sometimes denial and isolation breed anger and bitterness. We ask, "Why me? I don't deserve this." It often has an edge—anger at God. We know all the passages that promise God's help and care. But cancer bursts the bubble of our comfortable world where we rely on God's help and deliverance. We cry out, "God, why are you doing this to me? I'm a good mother or father. I love my family and take good care of them. Why, God?" We might concentrate on our pain and then compare ourselves with others, "It's not fair. So many others live happily without you. They never get cancer. Why me? Why give this to me? Why not those who don't trust you?" You're not alone! Psalm 73 also complains, "They have no struggles; their bodies are healthy and strong. They are free from common human burdens; they are not plagued by human ills. Surely in vain I have kept my heart pure" (Psalm 73:4,5,13).

In my own life, *without* cancer, I know how easily I can be overcome by the everyday irritations or problems that no one else in the world seems to know or understand. It's a dark place and a downward spiral. All alone . . . with my *self* . . . to focus on *self*—what I want things to be but what they are instead. What I'm going through that others will never have to go through. What I'm dealing with that others don't even know about or wouldn't even be concerned about if they did know. I want to cry. I want to say, "What about *me*? Just once I'd like it if someone would care about *me*."

I know firsthand that this self-pity can also touch those who have a loved one with cancer. "Does anyone care about this man who may lose his wife? Has anyone considered that maybe he too is scared and struggling and maybe feeling weak as well? Does anyone know how he is doing? Does anyone know that while his wife is crying on the outside, he is dying on the inside? No, I'm not the one with cancer, but I don't care. I'll say it: What about *me*?" To my shame, I confess that these selfish thoughts have been my own.

Then add cancer. Not my cancer but Linda's. I felt so helpless. I hurt too because of her trials. I sat with her as we heard the news. Her questions became mine. Her struggle became mine too. "Why us? Why the one I love? Lord, couldn't it be someone else?" Even anger: "Why punish us? It's not fair!" It all bubbled out of our combined selves. It wasn't my cancer. She felt the pain, denial, isolation, and anger at times. I was a step away as I watched and listened—helpless except for prayer and support. How often do loved ones also suffer in silence! Not only filled with concern for their loved one but also filled with questions and feelings that flow from the self. Maybe it's when everyone pays so much attention to the patient and nothing—apparently nothing—about the one who stands quietly in pain, doubts, and even anger like Ted Turner did at the death of his sister.

Do you remember how the Lord Jesus answered the question? We ask, "What about me? What about a little care for me? What about my happiness and my pleasure? What about my *self*?" And the loved one has similar questions: "What about us? Why give me this burden to share with her?" The Lord Jesus gave a shocking answer: "Whoever wants to be my disciple must deny themselves and take up their cross and follow me" (Mark 8:34). What about me? What about my *self*? Jesus gives it to us straight: "Cut off your relationship with your self-absorbed, self-loving *self* entirely. Disown your self-pitying *self* completely. Deny your self-focused *self* altogether. Yes, self-*denial*." You may ask, "Even now, when I've got cancer? Deny me, deny my . . . *self*, even now, when I'm so weak? What am I supposed to focus on in the pain . . . in the possible loss of my loved one?" Jesus responds, "Yes, even now. Even now. Just look again at my weak apostle Paul."

In the previous chapter we listened to Paul's review of the extreme hardships and weaknesses he had experienced in his service to the Lord and the Lord's church. Long hours and fatigue. Frequent imprisonment. Floggings and beatings. Stoning and shipwreck. In danger on the sea and in rivers. In danger from bandits and enemies of the gospel. Sleeplessness, hunger, thirst, nakedness, and exposure to the elements. If we didn't know better, we might say that Paul was on a pity trip, whining and feeling sorry for himself as he listed one trouble and hardship after another that had left him physically and emotionally tormented and so terribly weakened. We learned, however, that Paul was not on a pity trip.

Paul also lists one more pressure he had. He wrote, "Besides everything else, I face daily the pressure of my concern for all the churches" (2 Corinthians 11:28). What? No self-pity? No focus on his own suffering? The outward factors—fatigue, long hours, beatings, and persecution—were all secondary, just little and insignificant extras. In fact, if Paul had been asked, he would have said that those should not even be mentioned when compared to what weakened and burdened him most—what he describes as a "pressure." That was a strong word.

It's surprising that as weakened as Paul was by all of those external dangers and hardships, he was deeply focused not on himself but on others and their struggles. That's the kind of pressure Paul felt. He was deeply concerned for their faith. His was a deep and daily concern for the salvation of their souls. In the Corinthian congregation alone, Paul was extremely troubled that so many had been led away from the Savior by false teachings. He was incensed over a case of incest that the congregation, with apparent pride over its open-mindedness, had actually embraced (1 Corinthians chapter 5). He was distressed by the sinful factions and divisions in that church (1 Corinthians chapter 3), that the celebration of the Lord's Supper had become an unholy buffet (1 Corinthians chapter 11), and that the very heart of the Christian faith and that on which salvation hinges was being denied by some. Yes, Christ's physical resurrection from the dead was being denied by some (1 Corinthians chapter 15).

And this was just the church in Corinth. Paul was bombarded by issues and the urgent need for instruction and correction in so many other churches as well. They wrote letters to the apostle. They sent delegations to him. And all of this was his greatest load and challenge. Not the beatings, shipwrecks, or constant fatigue, but the pressure caused by his deep, constant, and anxious concern over the faith and salvation of his brothers and sisters in Christ. Paul wrote, "Besides everything else, I face daily the pressure of my concern for all the churches. . . . Who is led into sin, and I do not inwardly burn?" (2 Corinthians 11:28,29).

> Of the so many things that caused Paul to suffer, he allowed his deep concern for the souls of others to be his heartfelt concern.

Think about it. It's rather strange. Of the many things that caused Paul to suffer, he allowed his deep concern for the souls of others to be his heartfelt concern. It would have been reasonable if Paul, so wearied already by all of those outward troubles, had pined and whined, "Listen. I've got my own problems right now. My back is still tender and healing from the most recent 'forty lashes minus one' (2 Corinthians 11:24). My right ear is still plugged with saltwater after that last shipwreck. It's time to think about me." But amazingly he didn't.

To most people, it's a puzzling thing: that someone so beaten and weakened would be and could be concerned, first and foremost, about others—about *their* weakness. It's puzzling, . . . unless you understand what happens to people when they come to faith in Christ the Savior. What happens is truly glorious.

You see, when Jesus said, "Whoever wants to be my disciple must deny themselves" (Mark 8:34), he wasn't asking the impossible but instead fanning into flame what has already taken place in every believer. There's more to the Christian than meets the eye. A few years after Paul penned his second letter to the Corinthians, he wrote to the church in Ephesus, "You were

> "Whoever wants to be my disciple must deny themselves" (Mark 8:34).

taught, with regard to your former way of life, to put off your old self, which is being corrupted by its deceitful desires; to be made new in the attitude of your minds; and to put on the new self, created to be like God in true righteousness and holiness" (Ephesians 4:22-24). A new self! A different attitude. More like God than about yourself. But it's not magic or complete in this life.

Wouldn't it be a wonderful thing if, after becoming Christians, people would somehow lose their sinful, selfish, and self-centered nature, what Paul calls the old self? But that isn't the case. Christians must struggle against that nature every day for the rest of their lives. What is true is that at the very moment faith in Jesus the Savior is created in a person's heart, a new self is also created in that person. It is a new self with new thoughts and desires. It is a new self whose love for the Savior-God enables the Christian to want to do and be what God wants the Christian to do and be—"to be like God in true righteousness and holiness," to battle and put off the old self with its sinful and selfish self-centeredness and turn outward in love toward others.

That's what Paul experienced. The pressure and concern for others came because God had given him a new self. It is a new self with a new attitude of the mind, the completely selfless attitude of Jesus himself, "who, being in very nature God, did not consider equality with God something to be used to his own advantage; rather, he made himself nothing by taking the very nature of a servant, being made in human likeness. And being found in appearance as a man, he humbled himself by becoming obedient to death—even death on a cross!" (Philippians 2:6-8).

But it was a struggle for Paul as it is for every Christian. He wrote, "Although I want to do good, evil is right there with me. For in my inner being I delight in God's law; but I see another law at work in me, waging war against the law of my mind" (Romans 7:21-23). If you're a Christian, any Christian at all, even a Christian with cancer, this miracle has taken place in you. A new self. A new mind with a new and different attitude. And a new heart that is pumping with the love of Christ—his love *for* you and *in* you now enabling you, like Paul, even with cancer, to turn your loving attention and concern toward the souls of those around you. It's a struggle, however. We succeed and overcome the old self through Jesus Christ our Lord. We may not always win the battle against the sinful self, but we can always find forgiveness, strength, and hope in Jesus.

> "My flesh and my heart may fail, but God is the strength of my heart and my portion forever."

Remember Psalm 73 and the complaints about those who "have no struggles [and] are not plagued by human ills" (verses 4,5). The psalmist did not let the worries and doubts win. The psalmist concluded with a bold confession, "My flesh and my heart may fail, but God is the strength of my heart and my portion forever. But as for me, it is good to be near God" (verses 26,28). That's the new self winning the war. It happens because God's power has given the psalmist a new self. It happens because "it is good to be near God." Near to God! Listening to him. There is power. There is the boast—in the grace and hope God gives when we deny ourselves and set aside that old self.

I'm awed when I consider the selflessness of Paul in comparison to my own. I'm also ashamed. And then when I consider the total selflessness of my Savior—that Jesus, the Son of God, took the very nature of a humble and lowly servant for someone like me—I'm shamed more deeply. Yet that is not the reason or motive behind my selfless Savior becoming the humble servant. Not to shame or guilt me. But to free me from shame and guilt. To take all the ugly self-centeredness of my life upon himself and by his death pay for it in full. To forgive it completely. To turn this sinner into a saint before God. And to give me a whole new life to live—a life in which he nourishes my faith in him through his Supper and his Word and thereby dwells in me more and more.

> Yes, Christ himself is in me, more and more, empowering me to fight.

Yes, Christ himself is in me, more and more, empowering me to fight and kill the old self every day and constantly strengthening my new self so that amazingly, little by little, I look more like him. A little less selfish. A little more caring. A little less of the self-pitying "What about me?" and a little more concern for others. Less focus on what I'm going through and more attention to Linda and what she is going through—sympathizing with her struggles, understanding her very real need at times to cry on the outside, realizing her deep and constant need to crumble into the strong arms of the One who loves her more than I do, and then seeing to it that she does so.

I'm nothing special in this, and it's certainly not to my credit. It's due to a gracious God alone who has done this very same thing in the hearts and lives of countless millions. And again, if you're a Christian, any Christian at all, even a Christian with cancer, he's done it in you. A new self with a new mind and attitude that even now—in spite of all your weakness caused by the pain, the waiting, the fatigue, the uncertainty, the fear, the surgeries, the treatments, or the nausea—your new self is producing and prompting a deep concern for others, and especially for their souls, that may very well be the cause of your greatest and most painful weakness.

Even now, as difficult as it may be, you can wrestle for others in prayer and pray earnestly for those loved ones who may be struggling in their faith as they cope with the reality of your disease. You can muster the strength that will allow them to see Christ in you . . . even now when you're so weak. You can be certain they hear with their ears your unwavering trust that "in all things [even cancer] God works for the good of those who love him" (Romans 8:28). Your Lord has given you the strength to confess, "My flesh and my heart may fail, but God is the strength of my heart and my portion forever" (Psalm 73:26). A new self lives within you.

> You may swear you don't have the strength to do these things. Humanly speaking, you don't. But when you are at your weakest, Christ, living in you by faith, is at his best.

You may swear you don't have the strength to do these things. Humanly speaking, you don't. But when you are at your weakest, Christ, living in you by faith, is at his best—strengthening and empowering the new self through Word and sacrament and preserving in you something noble that to most may seem entirely out of place in the worst of times: a deep and loving concern for *others and their faith*. It's nothing short of miraculous. And like Paul, you can boast that the Lord has worked this miracle in you.

I mentioned in the first chapter a quiet drive to a hospital—quiet because my and Linda's hearts were heavy with uncertainty and dark possibilities. As I was considering this book, I asked Linda if she would be willing to peel back the veneer a bit and share some of her thoughts—things that were draining her and making her feel so weak. She did. She typed out a list, and I'm grateful. Let me share a sampling. Perhaps you can relate. "I have a headache that doesn't go away. Is the cancer going to my brain? When others ask if I've done the things on my bucket list. I seem fine today, but one infection might kill me. Am I going to get breast cancer too? When people tell me to slow down." And then there was this: "Showing my faith and trust in Jesus. I don't want to let my hair down somehow and thereby give my family or the people at church or the unbelievers at work an opportunity to be mad at God." And then this: "I want my funeral service to be the best-ever testimony to God's grace."

Funny thing, though. Look at her concern, even in the worst of times, for the faith and souls of others. She already is a testimony to God's grace! As am I! As was Paul! As are you!

Chapter 4
INSTRUMENT FOR GOOD

You may know someone like Leslie Lemke. I came across Leslie's story a number of years ago.

He was born prematurely with brain damage and cerebral palsy. His premature birth led to retinal problems and the surgical removal of his eyes at just a few months old. It took a year before he learned to chew; he was 12 years old before he learned to stand, 15 years old before he learned to walk; and he was always nonspeaking, unemotional, and distant.

But then one night his adoptive parents awoke to the sound of music. Thinking they had left the television on, they investigated and found Leslie playing the piano. It was Tchaikovsky's Piano Concerto No. 1, which Leslie had heard for the first time on television the night before and now performed flawlessly. Soon he was singing with a baritone voice and playing all styles of music—hearing the piece once and reproducing it perfectly.

I first learned of Leslie when I saw this man with no eyes on television singing, "Amazing grace—how sweet the sound—that saved a wretch like me! I once was lost but now am found, was blind but now I see" (CW 576). I remember how deeply touched and moved I was by seeing this blind man. And Leslie has touched and moved so many others, touring and sharing his music throughout the United States and overseas. God's work. Remarkable, isn't it? Remarkable that God would use a man so disabled, so physically, mentally, socially, and emotionally weak and lacking, to make such a positive impact and be such an instrument for good in the lives of others! Do you know someone like Leslie?

I don't know what cancer is doing to you. Maybe you're having one of those good days—feeling a little better, a little more energetic, and a little less sick and exhausted. But maybe it's not a good day. Maybe you're reading this in bed at home or in the hospital because you're just too weak to get up. If that's the case, then perhaps others are looking in on you: helping, taking care of your needs, and waiting on you. You're the recipient of their good. You may wish it were the other way around, that you could be an instrument for good in their lives. But right now you're just too weak. They are the ones who are making the positive impact.

> Even now you are a powerful instrument for good in the lives of others— an instrument of greatest good.

But things aren't always as they seem. That's especially true for Christians. Consider it *is* the other way around that even now you are a powerful instrument for good in the lives of others— an instrument of greatest good. Even now as you're being waited on—so physically and emotionally weakened by your disease— you are an instrument for good. Remarkable, isn't it? And true.

Recall that in the second letter to the Corinthians, Paul was compelled to defend himself and his ministry. Both had been scrutinized, belittled, and dismissed as weak and worthless by the false super-apostles. They had made their way into that congregation after Paul's departure and were seeking to replace his influence among God's people with their own. One of the charges of those false teachers—and apparently a charge to which many in the Corinthian congregation were nodding their heads—was that Paul was able to write letters to them that were filled with strongly worded admonition and stern calls to repentance, yet when the apostle was present with them, he was spineless and cowardly. He didn't have the courage, strength of character, or strong and persuasive speech consistent with what he had written. Sure, he could talk the talk when absent. That's easy! But he didn't have it in him to walk the walk when present. "His letters are weighty and forceful, but in person he is unimpressive and his speaking amounts to nothing" (2 Corinthians 10:10).

The super-apostles were ignorant of this shepherd's heart and his carefulness to deal gently and patiently with wayward sheep to guide them back into their Shepherd's arms. So their criticism was not so much over *what* Paul said when with the Corinthians but *how* he said it. "Meekly and weakly" was the charge. It was as if they chirped, "If Paul is really a chosen apostle and if Christ himself is really with Paul and speaking through him, there would be and ought to be some powerful demonstration of this—some strong and compelling proof." These super-apostles complained that they didn't see it, and some of the believers in the Corinthian congregation agreed.

Paul mentions another visit to the congregation, "This will be my third visit to you" (2 Corinthians 13:1). What the Corinthians and super-apostles were demanding—clear and powerful proof of Paul's apostleship—they would receive. Paul wrote, "I already gave you a warning when I was with you the second time. I now repeat it while absent: On my return I will not spare those who sinned earlier or any of the others, since you are demanding proof that Christ is speaking through me" (2 Corinthians 13:2,3). Paul will firmly and sternly deal with them

> The weaker Paul was, the clearer Christ's power could be seen in him.

and pronounce God's judgment. Yes, the Corinthians would get what they demanded; Paul would give them a show of strength.

Yet the apostle realized that his demeanor, whether strong and assertive or weak and unimpressive, had no bearing whatsoever on the truth that Christ was speaking through him. In fact, the weaker Paul was, the clearer Christ's power could be seen in him and his ministry. Paul went on to say, "[Christ] is not weak in dealing with you, but is powerful among you. For to be sure, he was crucified in weakness, yet he lives by God's power.

Likewise, we are weak in him, yet by God's power we will live with him in our dealing with you" (2 Corinthians 13:3,4). Paul was like the Savior whom he served—the Savior who willingly humbled himself and "was cruci-fied in weakness" yet was raised to life and "lives by God's power" to bestow the eternal riches of his saving work: forgiveness of sins and life eternal. The apostle's ministry was marked by a similar weakness and power. The weakness was pro-found. It was Paul's own. He was a fatigued and feeble, unimpressive and thorn-in-the-flesh-bearing servant. But the power was alien, outside of his weakness. It was the power of the almighty Son of God, Christ himself, speaking through this chosen instrument. Christ, speaking through Paul, was not weak in dealing with the Corinthians. The evidence was right before their eyes.

> It was the power of the gospel, what Paul called "the power of God that brings salvation to everyone who believes."

For indisputable proof of Christ's power in Paul's ministry, the Corinthians only had to look at themselves. How was it that they were Christians? How was it that they accepted and believed as truth the foolish gospel proclaimed by the weak and unimpres-sive preacher? How was it that their very hearts and minds had been changed so they had new, different, and noble thoughts and desires? How was it that they stepped out of the pattern of their culture and now fought against sexual immorality in their lives? And how was it that they were able to live every day, regardless of the day's circumstances, with a joy in their hearts that sprung from the certainty of their salvation? It wasn't due to Paul's charisma, eloquent words, or power of persuasion; the apostle had none of these. A higher power had to be at work. And it was!

You see, that was the power in Paul's life, seen all the more clearly when he was at his weakest. It was the power of the gospel, what Paul called "the power of God that brings salvation to everyone who believes" (Romans 1:16). That foolish gospel, even when proclaimed by the weakest of the weak, has explosive power to work inside a person and change that person forever. In the gospel the Savior himself comes. Softly. Tenderly. But with power. The power of the one with pierced hands and wounded side who gently calls sinners away from their dead-end lives. The power of him who hung on the cross until it was finished and who now speaks to the troubled conscience of a forgiveness that is real, full, free, and final. The power of him who destroyed the power of death and who embraces cold hearts, warming and winning them for a kingdom that has no end. It was and always will be the power of him who is love and who lovingly and powerfully works from the inside out, creating a new and wonderful way of life in each of his own—a life lived to the glory of God!

Remarkable—isn't it?—that a man as weak as Paul could make such a positive impact and be such an instrument for eternal good in the lives of so many others. That's the power of the gospel.

No, things aren't always as they seem. And again, that's especially true if you're a Christian. You see, here you are: weakened. It may be one of those good days, but maybe it's not. Maybe you're feeling weak like Paul and have never felt weaker in your life. Maybe you're embarrassed you can do nothing but be waited on and receive the kindnesses of others with nothing to give in return. If this is the case, I want you to understand that now—

> Now . . . is the time when you have the opportunity to make a real and eternal impact in the lives of others.

right now, when you are so terribly weakened in so many ways by cancer—is the time when you have the opportunity to make a real and eternal impact in the lives of others.

How? With the power in *your* life, the power that was in Paul's life—the power of the gospel. It is the power of Jesus himself who has come and still comes to you powerfully in his Word and sacrament. He's the one who leads you to recall the font where he swore to you, "You are mine! Forever!" and where he sent his Spirit to give you the faith that believes it is so. He's the one who speaks directly from the pages of the Bible to your needy heart of the perfect life he lived as your substitute. He comes to assure you of the eternal life and the resurrection to life that he promised. And he is the one who hosts a Supper for you—his body and blood together with the bread and wine, a feast of forgiveness and life, a teasing foretaste of the banquet that awaits you in heaven. And through all of these—and whether you feel it at the time—he strengthens your conviction that he is your Savior, deepens your trust in him, and fortifies your faith for whatever fight you have to face. That's the power of the gospel, the power in your life—even you, so weakened.

And it's with this power that you truly have the opportunity now to make a real and eternal impact in the lives of others. You see, this gospel of God's amazing grace does something wonderful inside a person. It creates hope. Life, of course, teaches us that hope can so often disappoint us. So we've learned to hope tentatively. But this hope of the Christian is different. This hope is actually a joyful expectation of the blessings ahead that the Christian knows with absolute certainty. It will take place. It is a wonderful conviction of the heart that the Lord Jesus will wrap us in his love in the future just as he has in the past. It is the unwavering confidence that he will use both good and bad times to bless and that he will give us every good blessing we need, even when we're forced to deal with disease and illness. And it is the certainty that when our time in this world is over, Jesus our Savior will send his angels to take us to be with him forever. There's nothing tentative about it, nothing uncertain, because this hope is based on what is reliable and true: the gospel of Christ.

> This gospel of God's amazing grace does something wonderful inside a person. It creates hope.

And where this *certain* hope is, there is another blessing: joy. Now don't confuse this with happiness. Happiness is dependent on circumstances, isn't it? We're happy when the bills are paid, we have our health, the kids are doing well in school, our friends are faithful, and our jobs bring satisfaction. Happiness is different than joy. It comes when our homes are filled with nice things and we're able to enjoy a vacation. But change the circumstances—take those things away—and happiness is gone.

What you have is much deeper, more solid. It's the joy of the Christian, joy that is present in spite of circumstances, joy that is there even when happiness is not. It's the inner peace, core of calm, and conviction of the heart that everything is fine because of Jesus. Everything is all right even through radiation, surgery, chemo, fatigue, and nausea. This joy sustains us in terrible weakness, unhappiness, and tears. Even then, everything is all right. Everything is all right, because Jesus loves you deeply, dearly, and eternally. That is solid. That will *never* change. And there it is: joy that cannot be destroyed.

And this is your power. It is the power of the gospel that has produced in you a hope and joy that cannot be diminished or destroyed by circumstances. This is the power, even now and whether you realize it, that is enabling you to make a powerful, positive, and eternal impact in the lives of others.

> It is the power of the gospel that has produced in you a hope and joy that cannot be diminished or destroyed by circumstances.

You see, you have something that so many others want. In a world that is desperately longing for a hope that won't disappoint, you have it. In a world that is running from one thing to the next, searching for a happiness that won't disappear when circumstances turn bad, you have a joy that is indestructible. And the people of the world will see it. They'll sense it. The technician who draws your blood. The neighbor who asks how you're doing. Those who sit in the waiting room with you. They'll sense it. They'll see it. Because it can't be hidden. And they'll know it's not an act or just false bravado. Your hope is real. So is your joy. And to so many, it's completely out of place. You should be going to pieces. You should be falling apart. You've got cancer! But here you are like a lighted match. In a lighted room, it's nothing. But turn out the lights, and the little match shines brilliantly. And so it is with you. Yes, the dark circumstances may make your light flicker a bit. But this is the time when the light of Christ and the light of your hope and joy in Christ are shining most brightly and brilliantly before

> This is the time when the light of Christ and the light of your hope and joy in Christ are shining most brightly and brilliantly before others.

others. They can't help but see and sense it because it can't be hidden even if you tried. They may even comment, "There must be something to this God you talk about." So tell them.

And all of this doesn't mean you'll always have a smile on your face. You have cancer. It's serious business. And it's sad. And like my wife, you may have the occasional meltdown. Limp and sobbing in my arms and so profoundly sad that it makes me uneasy. Yet I know the Lord has produced something in his daughter that cancer cannot destroy. I'll whisper, "Does he love you, Lin?" She still knows the answer. "Did he die for you?" She knows it's true. "Did he promise that he'd be with you, that he'd take care of you? Did he promise that no matter what happens, it'll be all right?" She knows. This weak one just needed to hear it again, and in doing so, she receives the power to wipe her tears and wash her face and move forward again in that certain hope and joy. And she does. It's hard for me to be objective about the woman I love, but she does. With an attitude, demeanor, words, and actions that don't fit her circumstances. Joyful and hopeful. And others do see it and sense it. Even comment on it. And then she tells them. And I know she tells them that it isn't her. Not at all. It's him. It's Jesus, giving and granting her the certain hope of a life that will never end and a joy that nothing can possibly destroy.

Remarkable—isn't it?—that God would choose and use such weak people as Leslie Lemke, Paul, Linda, and you to make such a positive impact and to be such instruments of eternal good in the lives of others! Yet it's when we're at our weakest that the Lord Jesus is at his best.

It's then that we can boast with the apostle, "When I am weak, then I am strong" (2 Corinthians 12:10). Because it's when we're weak that others can more clearly see and sense Jesus' power in us—the power of the gospel that keeps our hope and joy strong and reaches out to others with the same hope and joy.

Chapter 5
REFINED

God uses an interesting picture to describe his dealings with his people. Of course, he loves his people, but at times he has to refine them. Refining, or smelting, was the process by which metals were purified. A base metal ore would be placed into a blistering furnace until it reached its melting point. If it could have, I suppose the ore in the flames would have screamed or resented the process. Yet when it had reached a liquid state, something good happened: the dross, or the impurities, could be skimmed away. After the heat of refining, the metal was removed from the furnace. It was refined. It was stronger. Better. The gold was more precious. The copper pure. The silver more valuable.

You remember that the Israelites of the Old Testament were God's people. They were nothing special yet. Long before the Israelites even became a nation, God chose Abraham as the father of the nations. It was an act of pure grace. Then God made Abraham's descendants a great nation and delivered them from the slavery of Egypt. God chose them out of all the nations of the earth to be his precious possession. He tightly wrapped this people in his eternal love, made them the apple of his eye, blessed, and protected them. Above all, God, beginning with Abraham, swore to this people that from them and for them would come a Savior.

The Bible records the history of this people: so richly blessed by the Lord yet so consistently rebellious toward him. Like an adulterous wife, they gave themselves to other gods that they made with their own hands. They closed their ears to the voice of the Lord and instead listened to false preachers. Their worship of the

Lord had become nothing more than lip service, and the hypocrisy of their hearts revealed itself in every detestable form of evil in their lives. The almighty God of perfect justice who lives in unapproachable light and sparkles in unblemished holiness had every reason and right to destroy them.

But God would not. He remained faithful to himself and every salvation promise he had made. God chose to refine his people. Through his prophet Isaiah, he told them, "I will turn my hand against you; I will thoroughly purge away your dross and remove all your impurities" (Isaiah 1:25). God would do so by placing them "in the furnace of affliction" (Isaiah 48:10). His people would know the fire. It came in the form of hardship and economic loss. It came in the form of defeat and becoming a doormat for other nations. It came in the form of captivity and enslavement. Yes, the flames blistered their lives, pride, arrogance, and even their hopes for greatness in the world.

But the Lord's purpose was that of the refiner: to burn off the impurities of his people's unbelief and hypocrisy, purge them of false teaching, and eradicate the dross of the evil they had embraced. Frequently they didn't understand his loving purpose and, in fact, refused to see it as love. Frequently they rebelled against God and squandered his blessings. Yet those who humbly submitted to "the furnace of affliction" were not destroyed by it but refined by it.

> Those who humbly submitted to "the furnace of affliction" were not destroyed by it but refined by it.

When God delivered and removed them from the fire, they were better. Purer. Stronger. Through sorrow and pain, God had lovingly drawn them back to himself and preserved them as the people through whom and for whom the Savior would come. They were prepared to wait in faith for the coming of that Savior.

The Lord has not extinguished his refining fire. It continues to burn today and will burn until the end of time. He continues to use trouble, hardship, pain, and loss to purify his own, to burn away unbelief, self-righteousness, self-reliance, and sin. He purges his church and people of their fascination with false teaching and idolatry. Then he bestows on them some wondrous blessings that could come no other way but through the furnace of affliction and pain. As he sees fit, he may at times place more fuel on the fire than at other times. But he does this always in love for his people and always in faithfulness to and in the interest of his salvation promises.

Now you can guess where this is going. Like every Christian, you've known the fire in your life. You have been in the refining fire and felt loss, pain, heartache, or some sort of trouble. It hurt. You didn't like any of it. That's the fire. But God's love intended to make you better. When the dross was burned off, you were removed from the flames. Refined. Better. Blessed somehow, perhaps without you even realizing it.

But now you feel the fire of cancer. It's different, isn't it? Much more fuel on the fire. This isn't a summer cold, leaking dishwasher, or something else. This is cancer. The flames lick at every corner of your life and reach into the lives of others as well. If you belong to the Lord, then you know his promise in all of this. He promises all of it will be for your good. He may purge something. He may be preparing to

> There is no other way to receive this blessing from your loving Savior but by the fire of cancer.

give you some virtue or blessing. And yet in the rebelliousness inherent in all of us, you'd like to know the virtue or blessing the Lord has in mind and have the opportunity to refuse it. But no. He loves you too much and insists on giving it to you. Couldn't you just read about others with cancer and the blessings they received? No, that won't do. There is no other way to receive this blessing from your loving Savior but by the fire of cancer.

Whether it's you or a loved one with the disease, Jesus calls you to trust. He calls you to focus on his cross, to see his empty tomb.

Then seeing what he did for you, he wants you to know and trust that his love for you would never send you anything but good. "Take my hand," he gently says. "I love you. I'll be with you in the fire. Take my hand now. There is no other way to receive this treasure I have in mind for you. Take my hand."

We've been spending time reviewing the sufferings and weaknesses of the apostle Paul. It was in his second letter to the Christian congregation in Corinth that he wrote of floggings, beatings, stonings, shipwrecks, constant and deadly threats to his body and life, sleeplessness and fatigue, and his chronic "thorn in the flesh"—the "messenger of Satan" that tormented him (2 Corinthians chapters 11 and 12). Paul experienced all of these for the sake of Christ and his gospel ministry of Christ. Yet as painful as these were, they served as a refiner's fire. Paul was purged of conceit. Self-righteousness had been burned away. And so terribly weakened by his sufferings, he and others received the blessing of being able to clearly see and recognize a divine power behind Paul and his ministry. The weaker Paul was, the more he relied on Christ and the stronger he became in Christ.

But how would it all turn out? Paul didn't know at the time. Within a year of writing 2 Corinthians, he wrote another letter, this one to the church in Rome. In this letter Paul indicated that the Holy Spirit had somehow given him confidence that he would be able to fulfill his heartfelt desire to visit the Christians in Rome and that he would do so "in the full measure of the blessing of Christ" (Romans 15:29). In other words, Paul had received the assurance that the Lord would so arrange and direct affairs that the apostle's visit would be a blessing of richest measure both to Paul and to the Roman Christians as well.

Paul, however, would not visit Rome the way he wanted immediately. He informed those Christians, "Now, however, I am on my way to Jerusalem in the service of the Lord's people there. For Macedonia and Achaia were pleased to make a contribution for the poor among the Lord's people in Jerusalem. So after I have completed this task and have made sure that they have received this contribution, I will go to Spain and visit you on the way" (Romans 15:25,26,28).

Here's the interesting thing. One might think that Paul, like you perhaps, would be completely refined—a finished product entirely ready to deliver the offering for the poor to Jerusalem and then move on quickly to Rome. Not so. In fact, Paul himself realized that the Lord lovingly continues the refining of his own people until he takes them home to heaven. So he wrote to the Christians in Rome, "I urge you, brothers and sisters, by our Lord Jesus Christ and by the love of the Spirit, to join me in my struggle by praying to God for me. Pray that I may be kept safe from the unbelievers in Judea and that the contribution I take to Jerusalem may be favorably received by the Lord's people there, so that I may come to you with joy, by God's will, and in your company be refreshed" (Romans 15:30-32). Was more refining fire awaiting him?

Paul was not being paranoid but rather realistic about probable trouble and suffering that he would encounter at the hands of unbelievers in Judea. In fact, as he traveled toward Jerusalem, he had the opportunity to speak to the elders of the congregation in Ephesus, a city in Asia Minor. He told them, "Compelled by the Spirit, I am going to Jerusalem, not knowing what will happen to me there. I only know that in every city the Holy Spirit warns me that prison and hardships are facing me" (Acts 20:22,23).

The Holy Spirit's warnings became reality. A Jewish lynch mob in Jerusalem beat Paul and tried to take his life. He was rescued from that mob, but then he was arrested by the Roman authorities. He spent two years imprisoned in the port city of Caesarea. Then came his trials, the sea journey to Rome as a prisoner, the tempest, and the shipwreck. Finally, in Roman custody, he arrived at the capital.

When Paul wrote his letter to the Romans, these sufferings and hardships were still in his future. The Lord warned of prison and hardships ahead, but Paul wasn't told the extent and details of the troubles that awaited him. Yet he wrote with certainty about two things: He would visit his fellow Christians in the capital city, and when he came to them, even if it was as a prisoner, he would certainly come "in the full measure of the blessing of Christ." You see, Paul could make the connection. He understood and trusted that as the Lord directed affairs, he would allow his apostle to undergo further suffering and necessary refining. When he eventually arrived in Rome with the good news of Christ the Savior, his visit would be of the greatest possible benefit to both himself and his fellow Christians. That godly goal would be reached but only because Paul had come as a prisoner refined in the fire.

> The great challenge in all of this to Christian faith and trust is not knowing the details of the trials or even the outcome.

Of course, the great challenge in all of this to Christian faith and trust is not knowing the details of the trials or even the outcome. How hot must God make the fire and how much fuel is necessary in order to accomplish his intended work? How long must the metal stay in the flames and will the metal have to return to the flames? What is the particular dross that the refiner wants to burn away? What is the specific blessing that God wants to impart?

Paul was not privy to any of the details. We do not know them either. The Lord had not told him specifically about that bloodthirsty mob in Jerusalem, that lengthy imprisonment in Caesarea, or that life-threatening sea voyage. Nor had the Lord disclosed his loving intent and purpose behind each of these. While Paul may very well have been puzzled and confused, even troubled and challenged as he was led through each blaze, there remained deep inside a confidence that the fire was for his good, not his destruction. That confidence was not without foundation. Paul wrote to the Romans, "Since we have been justified through faith, we have peace with God through our Lord Jesus Christ, through whom we have gained access by faith into this grace in which we now stand. And we boast in the hope of the glory of God. Not only so, but we also glory in our sufferings, because we know that suffering produces perseverance; perseverance, character; and character, hope. And hope does not put us to shame, because God's love has been poured out into our hearts through the Holy Spirit, who has been given to us" (Romans 5:1-5).

You may want to read those words again. Do you see the connection Paul is making? Making for you? Before you gave God a thought, he gave you his Son. And before you gave the Son a thought, he gave you his perfect life and then his suffering and death, making the full and final payment for your sins by suffering your hell and dying your death. It is done! Then by rising to life, your Jesus gave you the solid assurance that through faith in him you have been justified and would rise again to eternal life. Like a judge in a courtroom, God has declared that you are *not guilty*—perfectly righteous and acceptable in his sight. As he did with Paul, the holy God has made real and eternal peace with you by forgiving your sins. You've been reconciled to him for time and eternity. In addition, you've been granted unrestricted access to the throne of the one who reigns over all things. You can freely and fearlessly voice all of your longings to him. And then there's even more. You may rejoice in the certain hope and anticipation of what your Savior-God has had in mind for you all along: sharing in his glory and the glories of his unending heaven.

> Whatever fire—even the fire of cancer—whatever suffering the Lord allows to touch your life, he does so in the same unparalleled love by which he justified you.

Here's the connection you'll want to make: Whatever fire—even the fire of cancer—whatever suffering the Lord allows to touch your life, he does so in the same unparalleled love by which he justified you and with the same heavenly goal he has in mind for you. Through fire and flame, he's always with you, always working toward that goal. Using suffering to temper and strengthen you and produce in you the quality of perseverance, of being able to bear up under hardship. And then a proven character follows, one that has known the fire and is able to withstand the next. Even if you cannot understand his ways or his particular management of your life, the refiner is dealing with you in love and with that goal of heaven in mind—blessing you somehow, blessing you even now.

I really can't put my finger on the particular blessings that have come to Linda and me through her illnesses. The refiner hasn't shared the details, but he has simply called us to trust. Looking back over the past few years, I can see that both Linda and I have been a little less caught up in the things of this life. We're financially stable, own a home and cars, and have kids and grandkids whom we love. We are blessed with friends who are so close that we would literally die for them and they for us. Both Linda and I could go on and, if not for cancer, could also easily get wrapped up in all of these. But the fire of cancer, the *blessing* of cancer, has burned away some of our focus on these good but fleeting things. We talk a little more freely now about death, dying, rising, and living. We talk a little more often now about heaven. We wonder what it will be like, what we will be like, and what God has in store for us. Our hearts burn within us with anticipation.

I've noticed too that some of the dross of self-centeredness and self-pity has burned away.

Cancer puts you in contact with so many others—some older, many much younger than yourself—who are also suffering with some form of the disease. Many of their trials are much more serious. You see them in the waiting room. The couple who has been married for 50-plus years. Her old head is wrapped in a scarf. He holds her hand. He just holds on, so afraid of losing her. You see the young woman, too young and frail, almost skeletal.

You wonder where her cancer has struck. Your heart breaks for her. You pray that all of them are not dealing with the disease without Christ.

For us, then, we wonder if the Lord has given us many other blessings and Christian virtues we have not yet realized. We know this God of ours is not a miser. He gives blessings that could come to us in no other way but through the fire. Yes, we have received blessings for certain, for "since we have been justified through faith, we have peace with God through our Lord Jesus Christ" (Romans 5:1).

And so it is with you, being refined and blessed somehow. Now it's difficult to see that when you're in the fire, isn't it? And so, through the flames of radiation, chemo, surgery, or the fear of losing someone you love dearly, I beg you to eye your Savior's cross—a Savior who loves you so deeply that he died for you so you might know and have the forgiveness of your sins, peace, and certain hope. As he revealed his plans to Paul to visit Rome without giving him the details, so without giving you the details, his plans for you are to bless you today, tomorrow, and for eternity. That's his promise to you, even through ways that puzzle and challenge you.

> Without giving you the details, his plans for you are to bless you today, tomorrow, and for eternity. That's his promise to you, even through ways that puzzle and challenge you.

I will not venture to tell you what God has in mind for you today. I simply don't know the exact purpose of his refining and the specific blessing coming your way. Perhaps the refiner has allowed you to see his intent to make you more heavenly minded, to instill in you a patience you never imagined you could muster, or to grant you new opportunities to share your hope and peace. Some of those opportunities come because of your cancer. You would never have them without it. In truth, it really doesn't matter if you can identify the refiner's details. What matters is that even now, in weakness and in spite of weakness, you have reason to boast with confidence. You have a God who has made solid and trustworthy promises to you about your future and will use all things along the way, even the fire, to refine you and bring you safely home.

"Take my hand now," he says.

Chapter 6
WHERE'S MY VALUE?

In 2015, I visited the traveling Vietnam Veterans Memorial Wall. Although roughly half the size of the wall in Washington, D.C., the names of more than 58,000 women and men who lost their lives in that conflict were there.

Wearied vets with lined faces proudly wore their uniforms and manned displays nearby. There were maps of Vietnam, black and white photos that preserved the violent and confusing time, and models of helicopters. A tiger cage that was used to hold US prisoners of war (POWs) was also there. The cage, constructed of bamboo, was perhaps 4 feet square and about 4 feet high. The placard said that POWs often spent months in the cage. *Months.* I was again astonished at what people are capable of doing to other people, and I was suddenly overwhelmed by a deep sadness. The vet standing nearby asked if I had any questions. I couldn't answer without my voice cracking. I shook my head no while trying to restrain tears.

As I drove home, I couldn't stop thinking about that cage. Even now I think about it from time to time. I think of the fear and dread of every POW because of it. For those held captive in it, I can imagine the utter helplessness and hopelessness of that confinement. They suffered the pain of having lost all freedom, even freedom of movement. All that was completely stripped away.

Cancer can be like that cage. In a very real sense, it can strip you of freedom—your freedom to go where you'd like and to do and enjoy what you'd like. You cannot do what you've planned. It will not allow you to follow your blueprint and agenda. That happens, of course, in everyday life. We don't always realize what we hope or plan for or what is on the day's agenda. The unexpected pops up, and we're forced to adjust. While it may cause some irritation and frustration, we've learned to deal with it. We've learned to expect the unexpected.

But cancer does more, doesn't it? Life—and quite often, every bit of life—is put on hold, and in the back of your mind, you know that life as you intend it may never return. Whatever you had planned may never become reality. You're no longer entirely free to move onward, to dream, to plan much of anything at all. You're bound and tied down by cancer. Your personal agenda means nothing now because your illness has its own agenda.

And much of that agenda dictates that you do nothing but wait. How long? Cancer won't tell you. The medical staff can give estimates, but cancer simply dictates, "Wait!" Often it's an agonizing wait. You may want to scream at someone, "What's taking so long? I can't take the wait." Yet you're held captive by it. Waiting for the diagnosis. Is it malignant or benign? Waiting to get another appointment with the oncologist. Waiting for the consultation with the surgeon. Waiting to get stronger. Waiting for the test results to come back. So much waiting without knowing when answers will come or what they will be. Waiting. Always waiting. Just the agonizing wait of cancer.

> With cancer, we agonize with the frequent inability to live our lives with that former sense of value or purpose.

With cancer, we agonize with the frequent inability to live our lives with that former sense of value or purpose. To do so, of course, is vital to our existence. It's how we're built. You see, a time comes in every person's life—sooner for some, later for others—when we realize an inherent need to accomplish something and to do something of significance. It's how we're built. It's in our DNA. We become the nurturing mother, the strong father, the do-it-yourselfer around the house, the organizer, the one at work on whom others often depend. We take responsibility and become the one others can count on to get the job done. We find great fulfillment and satisfaction in living what we are. In fact, a gnawing restlessness and disappointment make us feel worthless if we don't or can't do it.

Perhaps that's where you are—feeling caged. You are sick and tired of being sick and tired with cancer. If you are the parent, child, spouse, or friend of a sick and tired victim of cancer, you too are somewhat sick and tired of it— though you would never confess that out loud. "What happened to my friend, the vibrant, energetic friend I used to know? What happened to my wife? My husband?" Maybe it's you with the disease asking, "What happened to the old me?"

> You are sick and tired of being sick and tired with cancer.

We all have moments when we feel we're simply taking up space and time, making no significant impact on the world around us. But those moments pass. We pick ourselves up and go about our business and make ourselves useful again. To do so is a good thing. But what if you *can't* pick yourself up? You're too weak to get out of bed by yourself, too weak to shower or use the washroom by yourself, and just too tired and worn out to do much of anything. To a large extent, you become dependent on others even for the basics. All of the accomplishments, all of the being needed by others, all of the real value and worth of you being *you* in this world and in the lives of others—all of that is gone. "I don't want to be helpless; I want to be the helper. I want my life to continue to mean something. I don't want to be a burden and waited on. But I'm caged." How difficult and agonizing that can be.

At the time, Linda's leukemia was under control, and she was active, taking care of our home, serving faithfully in our church, and working at her job where she was respected and had a position of responsibility. Then uterine cancer and surgery changed that for a time. Eventually she was diagnosed to be cancer-free.

Sweet music to her ears and the ears of everyone. But shortly thereafter, she felt a lump. The mammogram was inconclusive. A biopsy was taken and sent to the Mayo Clinic. We waited and, yes, feared the worst. Perhaps Linda was thinking, "One way or another this cancer stuff is going to kill me." In a moment of deep sadness she sobbed, "When I'm gone, I don't want my grandkids to remember me as their sickly grandma who was always in bed and always too tired to do anything with them."

> A life that is suddenly without value and purpose can be empty, agonizing, and purely miserable.

A life that is suddenly without value and purpose can be empty, agonizing, and purely miserable. Perhaps you know this. The apostle Paul knew it too. You recall that Paul's purpose in life had been made clear to him by the Lord Jesus himself: Go with the gospel to the Gentiles and proclaim to them the good news about Christ their Savior. So Paul went. He went boldly, energetically, and enthusiastically, preaching and teaching the gospel of Jesus. Crisscrossing the eastern Mediterranean world, he established Christian churches and strengthened the faith of his fellow believers through his letters.

But then came a visit to Jerusalem with an offering for the poor. As Paul had predicted, unbelieving Jews stirred up trouble against him, riling a frenzied mob in the temple that attempted to beat the Lord's apostle to death. Only the Roman commander and his troops squelched the uproar and stopped the vicious attack. In the confusion, Paul was arrested and jailed. But his enemies' hatred would not subside until they carried out a plot to assassinate the apostle even while in Roman custody. That plot was discovered, and Paul, for his safety and under heavy Roman guard, was transferred by night to the port city of Caesarea and found a new prison waiting for him.

There Paul sat for two years confined in the official headquarters of the Roman governor Felix. For reasons we do not know, the feverish pen of the Lord's missionary was set aside. He was confined and all his mission travels stopped. It is true that Paul's imprisonment was similar to house arrest and that Felix allowed Paul "some freedom" and some interaction with "his friends" who were permitted "to take care of his needs" (Acts 24:23). But how difficult this period of near inactivity must have been for Paul! How agitating for Christ's energetic "chosen instrument to proclaim [Jesus'] name to the Gentiles and their kings" (Acts 9:15)!

The Scriptures tell us that Felix "sent for [Paul] frequently and talked with him." Without a doubt, Paul took those opportunities to tell the governor about Jesus, but it seems that the governor was not so much interested in his Savior as he was in being offered a bribe from Paul for his release (Acts 24:26). The Scriptures also tell us that Paul was given an opportunity to speak about Jesus to Felix's successor, Festus, together with that governor's guests, King Agrippa and his sister Bernice (Acts chapter 26). Was he given further opportunities to do so? Perhaps. We just don't know. Yet we can say with confidence that Paul's life as he had known it was put on hold.

> God himself has placed a value on you that is beyond your comprehension so that you might be of value to him and others.

There's a very good chance that, to one degree or another, you might also feel Paul's restlessness and frustration. You may understand well the search for something that gives meaning to your existence now. But you can't. Cancer has confined you, and now your life seems to have diminishing value. Everything you have known and done has been put on hold indefinitely. What's your purpose *now*? Perhaps, as with Paul, you can only guess.

I want to remind you of something. Please take this to heart: God himself has placed a value on you that is beyond your comprehension so that you might be of value to him and others. Paul wrote, "It is by grace you have been saved, through faith—and this is not from yourselves, it is the gift of God—not by works, so that no one can boast" (Ephesians 2:8,9). You see, this is the value God has placed on you. It is an entirely undeserved favor. He offered up his own Son so he might have you as his own forever. You are saved by God's grace alone through Jesus' life, death, and resurrection from the dead. In addition, he has given you the faith that trusts Jesus and makes this salvation yours. Because of those gifts, he has provided a life for you now of value and purpose. Paul continued, "We are God's handiwork, created in Christ Jesus to do good works, which God prepared in advance for us to do" (Ephesians 2:10). That's the life—a life of good and meaningful works flowing from a heart that wants to do them. He has that in mind for all his people. He simply will not allow cancer, weakness, and the difficult confinement and inactivity that often come with cancer to strip you of that value and purpose.

I don't have the answers to what your God has in mind for you now. Sometimes, whatever our circumstances, we have to look for the purpose he intends. But let me suggest a few things.

I picture Paul, confined in Caesarea for two years, doing a lot of praying. More than likely he had plenty of time to pray. I see the wearied apostle with folded hands and bowed head praying for himself, his life, his safety, and his freedom. I hear him pleading with the Lord Jesus that he might somehow continue to be that "chosen instrument" proclaiming salvation in Christ to a world that desperately needed to hear it (Acts 9:15). I see Paul praying for that world and so many others he knew and did not know. In fact, read Paul's letters in the New Testament and you'll discover a man who seems to have relished the opportunity to pray for others. He prayed that they would come to faith, that God would strengthen their faith, that he would help them live the blessed life of faith. I picture Paul praying to the God of limitless grace and power who hears and answers the prayers of his people. No, Paul's life had not been stripped of its value because of his confinement.

Neither has yours. Perhaps, unlike Paul, you're not one of those Christians to whom prayer comes easily. You don't necessarily relish the opportunity. It's not your greatest gift, but instead you have to work on it. So work on it. Discipline yourself if need be. Schedule it if need be. Like Paul, perhaps you have the time for it now. So pray. Pray for yourself, your life, and your health. Pray for others as well. Pray for those whose lives are being touched by your illness. Pray for *their* health, *their* strength, and *their* comfort. Above all, pray for their faith in the living Lord Jesus. As you do, please see and know with certainty that even now your life in Christ has not been stripped of its value. In Christ, that's impossible.

> Pray for yourself, your life, and your health. Pray for others as well.

Let me make another suggestion. I see Paul there in Caesarea serving. Yes, in a very real sense he served as the recipient and object of the Christian love and concern of those friends who were permitted "to take care of his needs" (Acts 24:23). Granted, this may be a hard pill for many to swallow. It is not easy to be passive, need help, and allow yourself to be helped rather than to be the one helping. It takes a special kind of inner strength to fulfill this purpose of the Lord. And yet it is the Lord himself who gives and grants that strength—the amazing strength to be the object of others' love and concern. Listen to the Lord as he speaks to you in his Word, repeats his unbreakable promises, and gives you the ability to be something that formerly was foreign to you: a recipient instead of a giver. You may be the recipient of care and the beneficiary of others' help. Yet realize what the Lord is allowing you to be: one whose life is of such great value now because it is giving others the opportunity to do this good work that God prepared in advance for them to do.

I don't know what the Lord has in mind for Linda. Or me. Perhaps someday she will be that sickly grandma in bed, too tired to play with her grandkids. Yet if that happens, she will be a sickly grandma of such unique and wonderful value for her grand-kids. She will be the recipient. She will be the one for whom they will construct even more homemade cards than they do today. They will hand her watercolor paintings of Jesus, his Christmas manger, his Good Friday cross, and his empty Easter tomb, each with an "I love you, Gramma" scrolled on the front. What value her life will have! Even then, if that happens, what a glorious purpose to serve as the outlet to actively express their faith-born yearning to serve their Savior. Tough as that might be, she'll be able to handle it. She will actually rejoice in it. Because Jesus will give and grant that strength to her too as he speaks tenderly to her heart, repeats his gracious promises, and, yes, also gives her the ability to do something that has been foreign to her.

That leads to a final suggestion. As Jesus speaks to you in his Word and draws you closer to him, you will know a renewed desire to carry out an old but unsurpassed purpose: to talk with others about him. You have unique opportunities to do so today. I see Paul, for instance, talking about the Savior to people he never would have met if not for his imprison-ment. Because of cancer, you're no doubt meeting a lot of people you never would have met if not for your disease: the greeters at the clinic, the roommates in the hospi-tal, the scared and hurting members in your support group, and the kind people who give you loving care and concern. Is this it? Are you perhaps God's special and chosen instrument who, like imprisoned Paul, has been given new opportunities to tell another person about the Savior? Please consider it. It could be. We'll talk more of this in the next chapter.

> From start to finish, you are the workmanship of the Savior and that means your purpose and value *cannot* be stripped from you.

It's understandable that you may be struggling to see your full value and purpose today. The confinement and diminished activity of cancer will do that. Yet from start to finish, you are the workmanship of the Savior and that means your purpose and value *cannot* be stripped from you. Nothing, not even cancer, can destroy it. The Lord may be tweaking the ways in which you impact the lives of others, and you may have to look hard for new and unexpected opportunities to serve him. Yet you can boast. As weak and confined as you are, you can boast that nothing can destroy your value. God has declared it so by the cross of his Son.

Chapter 7
EVEN NOW, SHARING JOY

I have never met Kia. She's an X-ray technician at a local hospital. Linda's cancer and CLL have brought her into contact with Kia on a handful of occasions. Even though their meetings have been somewhat infrequent and relatively short, a bond has formed between the two. I first sensed it when Linda got home after a CT scan talking about Kia and her warmth and genuine concern. Kia's mother had recently died after being diagnosed with breast cancer that was already in stage 4, but Kia told Linda that it was Jesus who was granting her strength in her time of pain. She confessed that in her sudden loss, Jesus was filling her with peace in her time of weakness. Linda and Kia talked about him so that, even though Linda had just received a scan that was looking for more bad and deadly stuff inside, she arrived home well and happy. No, it wasn't *happy*; there was *joy*. She so appreciated being able to talk with someone who understood that because of Jesus, "this is just for now; this is not forever." She was strengthened having talked about Christ. I'm guessing that Kia was strengthened too. I wish I had been with them.

> She so appreciated being able to talk with someone who understood that because of Jesus, "this is just for now; this is not forever."

That bonding of sisters in Christ and those warm expressions of heartfelt concern would not have happened without cancer. Chances are the two would not have met until heaven if not for cancer. It's more than just the bonding of sisters who share challenges. They talked about Jesus. The strengthening of each other in the faith and in the joy and peace that surpass understanding is a special bond in life's journey through troubled times.

There have been others. We've met and have come to know so many others whom we most likely would never have met if not for Linda's health. The circle of our acquaintances has expanded. We now see oncologists, surgeons, insurance helpers, nurses, receptionists, and an incredibly friendly Nigerian greeter at the cancer center who still has a little difficulty with English. Some we've gotten to know on a first-name basis.

Because of cancer, we've even bumped into people we haven't seen in years. As we were sitting in the reception area of the cancer center waiting to have Linda's blood work done, I noticed a young woman in her late 20s or 30s who was also waiting. I turned to Linda and softly asked, "Is that Tammy?" Now I had not seen Tammy in years, and how in the world I had been able to recognize her I don't know. But Linda recognized her as well and confirmed, "It *is* Tammy." I walked over and reintroduced myself. And while Tammy also recognized me, it was obvious she was having a particularly bad day and hard time and did not want to chat. Cancer will do that.

The following day I decided to reconnect with Tammy's mom, Rachel. I had not seen her in years either. I phoned and let her know that I had seen Tammy at the cancer center and hoped that her daughter was doing well. Rachel asked if we could get together to talk. When we did, this hurting mom poured out her pain. A young daughter had cancer. Another young daughter was recently killed in a boating accident. So much hurt. So much anger. So much confusion. She wanted to know why. I had no answers. But I did have peace for her broken heart and soul and joy for her troubled life. I took her to the cross—to that amazing love of Christ her Savior. I encouraged her to fall into his arms. I invited her to worship. Two weeks later she was there.

But it would not have happened—none of these things would have happened—if not for cancer. To strengthen a fellow Christian in her faith and trust in the Savior and be strengthened in return is a joy. Sharing the healing balm of Jesus' saving love with an aching and shattered mother lifts not only her heart but also yours. It brings a sense of joy that not even a deadly disease can destroy. None of these marvelous things would have happened and none of these lives, most likely, would have been touched for good if not for cancer. That kind of changes your view of cancer, doesn't it?

> To strengthen a fellow Christian in her faith and trust in the Savior and be strengthened in return is a joy.

Let me digress a bit. I think of George Bailey in *It's a Wonderful Life*. Every year I watch and get caught up in his desperation and despair over a life that he is certain has meant nothing to anyone. But I always do so knowing that at the end, everything turns out all right. At the end of the movie, they always sing, "Glory to the newborn King." Because of Christ the glorious King, everything does turn out all right. He has promised that "though [we] walk through the darkest valley, [we] will fear no evil" (Psalm 23:4). We have eternal life waiting for us.

Let's look at the movie again. Between George's desperation and that delightful ending scene, you may recall that he receives a unique gift from Clarence, his guardian angel. In spite of the obvious fantasy, it's an intriguing thought for all of us: "What would my world be like if I had never been born?" The story allows George to see it. He sees that without him, his charming little hometown of Bedford Falls has become Pottersville, filled with booze, sleaze, and hardship. The pretty little homes that common folk were able to finance because of George's Building and Loan have been replaced by slums. George's absentminded but lovable Uncle Billy ends up in a home that cares for mental patients. George's brother, Harry, who saved the lives of many soldiers and became a decorated war hero, drowned as a boy when he fell through thin ice. Because George had never been born, he was not there to save him so those whom Harry saved during the war were also dead. Bewildered, George sees it all. He sees what his world would be like if he had not been born. Clarence provides the lesson: "Strange, isn't it? Each man's life touches so many other lives. When he isn't around he leaves an awful hole, doesn't he?"

You've got to agree with that. Our stories are different, though. We never get to see what our lives would be like if we had not been born. But spend a little time thinking about that. As you deal with cancer—in fact, *especially* now as you deal with cancer—you would leave an awful hole if you were not around. Perhaps you haven't given it a thought, but your life today has touched and is touching so many others. Children, spouse, and friends would all have different lives or not even exist if you were not there. Think of those you touched because of your disease. Think of all the people you've met, know today, and bumped into again only because of your illness. If you do nothing else, make a list. Incredible, isn't it?

> Your life today has touched and is touching so many others.

But now consider this as well: God has allowed the weakness of your cancer to give you special and unique opportunities to encourage and strengthen others. You may not always be strong enough to do it, but you can encourage and be encouraged by those God places in your life. You can fill the real, awful hole of those you meet who are still searching for that something in life. In spite of cancer, you can share the indestructible peace, hope, and joy that are yours with so many who are still living in darkness and despair. All of these marvelous things are only possible *because* of cancer and the insight you have about your Savior, life, and cancer. That changes your view of the disease, doesn't it?

Paul's sufferings gave him the same sort of unique and special opportunities. Toward the end of his rather quiet two-year imprisonment in Caesarea, it became obvious to Paul that he would never receive a fair trial in that city or, as proposed by governor Festus, back in Jerusalem where the apostle was first arrested. Paul, therefore, exercised his right as a Roman citizen. He appealed his case directly to Emperor Caesar. Before long, Paul was on a ship headed for Rome. But things would not get better soon.

> God has allowed the weakness of your cancer to give you special and unique opportunities to encourage and strengthen others.

Aboard the ship Paul met people he had never met before and would not have met if not for his imprisonment and sufferings. Other prisoners, who apparently had appealed to Caesar as well, were with him. A Roman centurion named Julius and his soldiers had charge of the prisoners. Of course, the ship's pilot and crew were there with Paul. After sailing past Cyprus, Julius, who belonged to the Imperial Regiment, transferred the passengers to an Alexandrian cargo vessel headed for Italy. Paul could have passed some time by making a list of the people he met only because of his hardships. Instead, the apostle used the time and opportunity to share his faith in the living God with his new acquaintances.

But the ship had difficulty making headway and lost time on its journey. The winds were against it, and the ship with its prisoners finally came to Fair Havens on the southern coast of Crete. It would not be a fair haven. The centurion would have waited out the weather there, but the harbor was unsuitable. Finally, a gentle wind gave the crew hope to sail for a safer harbor. After they sailed, the winds turned into a northeaster with hurricane winds. The ship was tossed and battered for days until any hope of survival was lost.

Contending with the howling wind, Paul raised his voice to the other 275 men aboard,

Men, . . . I urge you to keep up your courage, because not one of you will be lost; only the ship will be destroyed. Last night an angel of the God to whom I belong and whom I serve stood beside me and said, "Do not be afraid, Paul. You must stand trial before Caesar; and God has graciously given you the lives of all who sail with you." So keep up your courage, men, for I have faith in God that it will happen just as he told me. (Acts 27:21-25)

A few days later, as shipwreck loomed, Paul strongly urged those aboard to eat something with him; they would need their strength if they were to survive the wreck. Paul took his own advice but only after confessing his faith again by openly offering a mealtime prayer of thanksgiving to God in the presence of all of them.

Then the Alexandrian vessel was torn apart on one of the beaches of Malta, a small island south of Sicily. As God had promised, Paul and all of his new acquaintances survived safely. They stayed three months there, and Paul met many others whom he would not have met if not for the storm and shipwreck. Among them were the natives of the island as well as the chief officer there. Paul had new opportunities to share the hope Jesus offers to all. By the power of Jesus, Paul healed and then, no doubt, proclaimed the real power behind the healing. As he had done before, he made sure the people knew that the power was not his own but Christ's, the Savior of the Maltese people. If not for Paul's suffering and hardships, there would have been no healing or comfort from the Savior.

> If not for Paul's suffering and hardships, there would have been no healing or comfort from the Savior.

More than half a year after the journey began, Paul arrived in Rome. The appeal process to Caesar dragged on for over two years, yet it was not wasted time for the apostle. While it is true that Paul was a prisoner during that period and keenly felt the hardship of being confined, the terms of his incarceration were fairly lenient. He was fastened to a guard with a light chain and allowed to carry on a relatively normal schedule in his imprisonment. So Paul again took the opportunity to welcome fellow believers, including friends and coworkers with names like Timothy, Luke, and Epaphroditus. He gave and received strength, comfort, and joy in the Savior. He welcomed a runaway slave named Onesimus, told him about Jesus, and then wrote a letter to the slave's owner, Philemon, informing him that his slave had become a brother in Christ. Paul sent Onesimus back to his master, urging Philemon to receive his servant back in love and forgiveness.

Paul wrote other letters. We have many of them in the Bible—including one to the church in Ephesus and another to the church in Colossae. To the church in Philippi he wrote about the blessing that came from his troubles, "I want you to know, brothers and sisters, that what has happened to me has actually served to advance the gospel. As a result, it has become clear throughout the whole palace guard and to everyone else that I am in chains for Christ" (Philippians 1:12,13). You can almost see Paul filled with joy as he wrote those words. The Lord had so used the difficult and seemingly negative events in Paul's life to bring about the greatest good: the proclamation of the gospel. Even the hardened Roman soldiers who guarded Paul on a rotating basis had become familiar with his case and the message he proclaimed. They had been softened by it—so much so that they spoke about it to their families and others, who in turn spoke about it to still others. And the good and joyous news of the Savior spread. Even then, as Paul was limited by chains and confinement, his joy spread.

Paul noted one more positive development beyond his letters. Unexpectedly, the love of God touched even *more* lives. Paul continued, "Because of my chains, most of the brothers and sisters have become confident in the Lord and dare all the more to proclaim the gospel without fear" (Philippians 1:14). The apostle's courage and work, even while in chains, emboldened the Christian men and women of Rome to step out of the shadows and courageously identify themselves with Jesus Christ. You can imagine them saying, "Yes. I'm one of his," and then boldly proclaiming him to others. The joy of knowing Jesus and his promises spread, and Paul's personal joy in Christ was deepened by seeing it.

Does all of this sound like boasting on Paul's part? Well, it was! But this man of God wasn't boasting that he had somehow outwitted those who tried to silence him and halt his work. Rather, Paul was boasting in the Lord. He was boasting that his God had reversed all the negatives, as he always does. God had used the storm, the shipwreck, the imprisonment, and the frustrating delays in the appeal process to have Paul meet these people, old friends and new acquaintances, and—in spite of his severe hardships—to continue his life's purpose and passion of proclaiming Jesus the Savior. Paul knew that while he could be chained, God's saving Word can never be chained (2 Timothy 2:9). He knew and believed the truth that God has all things—*all* things—work together somehow for the good of his people and his kingdom (Romans 8:28). Paul's joy in the God of his salvation increased.

> God had used the storm, the shipwreck, the imprisonment, and the frustrating delays in the appeal process to have Paul meet these people.

I pray that, especially at this time in your life now, you can find an extra measure of that same joy. As a Christian, that joy is in fact already yours. Even now as you deal with your own or another's cancer, you have God's promise of his love, care, forgiveness, and eternal life. You see, it's not simply a matter of being happy. It's pretty difficult—isn't it?—to be happy when you're facing surgery or more treatments; when you're nauseated, numb, or too weak to go to work or fix a meal; when you're so chronically tired that all you want to do, or can do, is sleep, and then you wake to more exhaustion; or when you're watching someone whom you care for deeply, whom you love intensely, deal with the disease. It's pretty hard to be happy at such times.

But even in these times, joy is still there. It's still there. Beneath the sadness, weakness, and tears, it's still there. It's a genuine joy—a joy that is solid, certain, and unshakable because it isn't based on the changing experiences and circumstances of life or your treatment. It is built on a solid, certain, and unshakable Savior. You see, it's an *inner* joy—a trait, a quality in your character produced by the Holy Spirit of God. It's the indestructible joy that comes from knowing where you stand with the almighty God today, tomorrow, and forever because of his Son, Jesus. It's the calm confidence that has been given to you and knows the answers to Paul's questions: "If God is for us, who can be against us?" No one! "Who will bring any charge against those whom God has chosen?" No one! "Who then is the one who condemns?" No one! "Who shall separate us from the love of Christ?" (Romans 8:31-35). No one! Nothing! And in that, an indestructible joy looks forward to glory. You can say even in your weakness, "This cancer stuff is just for now. This is not forever."

> An indestructible joy looks forward to glory.

Now there's a peculiar restlessness in people who are filled with the joy of their salvation in Christ, and maybe you've noticed it in yourself. They need to have others know and experience that same unequaled and indestructible joy. There is, in fact, joy in seeing that happen. That was Paul, wasn't it? No doubt that's you as well. So I encourage you to take the opportunities you've been given because of cancer—those new and unexpected opportunities. Paul's life had been changed so he could no longer trek across the Mediterranean world and share Jesus with others. He was confined and limited. Your life too has been dramatically changed. But I'm certain your need and desire to share your joy in Christ has not. Take the opportunities. After considering it, I've learned that those new opportunities are more numerous than I can imagine. Look around. Make that list. See that mother whose heart is breaking over her daughter's cancer. Tell her about the joy that fills your heart and life even now. It is a joy for everyone. See your Kia. Let her encourage you and increase your joy in Jesus, and you do the same for her. See those who, like you, may be hurting and uncertain. Tell them that you understand because you really do. You've been there. Then tell them where you find strength, peace, and joy. Especially joy. Tell them about Jesus.

> See those who, like you, may be hurting and uncertain. Tell them that you understand because you really do. . . . Tell them about Jesus.

Isn't it remarkable how this God of ours works? Even when we are at our very weakest, he arranges things so we can be of the greatest possible good to others. He reverses and turns the negatives upside down. You probably never envisioned or considered that happening in your life today. Your God—so gracious, so loving—gives you so many opportunities to have your joy deepened by sharing it with others and changing a life for eternity all because of cancer. Yes, it really does change your view of the disease, doesn't it?

As with Paul, you can boast in that. Your joy will be deepened. Even now.

Chapter 8
IN THE END, VICTORY

The leaves always change color in fall. Soon they drop.

Of the 13 letters in the New Testament that come from the pen of the apostle Paul, his second letter to Timothy was the last written. The letter is from a loving spiritual father to his "dear son" in the faith (2 Timothy 1:2)—a young pastor whom Paul had chosen as a coworker and with whom Paul had a special bond. In the letter Paul reveals his heart that harbored a deep concern for Timothy as well as one for the future of the Lord's church. Paul strongly and repeatedly urges the young minister whom he loves to remain faithful and proclaim nothing but the truth of God's saving Word.

Among other things, the letter shares two things that may be of special interest to you, especially now at this time in your life. The apostle writes about loneliness and death.

Let's explore what we know about Paul after his two-year imprisonment in Rome. Because of his appeal to Caesar, we can say with near certainty that his appeal was heard and he was released. The missionary apparently picked up where he had left off—traveling the Mediterranean, proclaiming Jesus as Savior, visiting established churches, and strengthening fellow Christians in their faith. There is also some evidence that Paul realized his desire to journey with the gospel as far west as Spain (Romans 15:23,24).

At some point, perhaps four years or so after that first imprisonment, Paul was in the capital city again as a prisoner. We don't know why, but perhaps the persecution of the Christian church had become more intense. Whatever the circumstances, Paul was once again jailed. But it was different. Paul had no lenient confinement. This time Paul was "chained like a criminal" (2 Timothy 2:9), and he expected to be put to death because of his faith (2 Timothy 4:6). That happened.

For a moment imagine him: an old man weakened and worn by years of suffering. His body bore the ugly marks of the beatings he endured. He sat in a dark and damp cell with heavy chains that restricted his movements. The Romans imprisoned him for no other reason than that he proclaimed the truth about Jesus being the Savior of the world. Held secure by the chains, Paul was isolated and alone. The prison confinement kept most people away. Loneliness for this normally active missionary plagued him. It was a dreadful thing.

Paul had known many dark times in his life, some of them when he was actually abandoned and forgotten. So it was at the end, chained and imprisoned in Rome and nearly alone. Paul wrote that "only Luke," his dear friend and coworker, was with him (2 Timothy 4:11). This time the isolation was worse because the terms of Paul's confinement were much harsher than those of his first imprisonment. Maybe it was worse for him because it came after the good news of his first release. Now again he was in a Roman prison with little hope of release. Can you identify with that? You come back again for treatment after you have had good news. Now you're back where you were—only it's worse this time.

Those who would normally come to visit Paul either could not or chose not to visit for fear of being imprisoned for their own faith in Jesus. Whatever the situation, Paul was left lonely and yearning for the company and love of fellow believers. He urged and pleaded with Timothy, "Do your best to come to me quickly, for Demas, because he loved this world, has deserted me and has gone to Thessalonica. . . . Get Mark and bring him with you" (2 Timothy 4:9-11). "So come, Timothy," Paul pleaded. "I need you." Timothy read between the lines: "I'm alone and lonely."

But Paul was clear, "You know that everyone in the province of Asia has deserted me, including Phygelus and Hermogenes" (2 Timothy 1:15). It certainly wasn't by choice that Paul was alone in his sufferings and lonely.

Loneliness is a dreadful thing, isn't it? Perhaps you've experienced it in your journey with cancer—a loneliness deeper than that of Paul. It's not that others deliberately stay away, but perhaps they somehow retreat emotionally or socially. They might withdraw somehow because things are . . . well, . . . different. A friend's or loved one's cancer diagnosis can leave people feeling uncomfortable. What can they say, if anything? What can they do that hasn't already been done? While charity toward those people is in order, their withdrawal can leave the cancer patient feeling deserted and alone—bearing the burden alone and wondering, "Where is my support?" Even if you are given the opportunity to talk to others, it is impossible for them to fully understand. In the end, the cancer is not theirs but yours. You feel a definite isolation in bearing it. You are alone with the struggle, alone in front of the mirror, and alone with the fears and probabilities. You are lonely in all of this.

> Being alone and lonely *is* a dreadful thing. Yet even in this, the people of God are blessed like no other and can actually boast that they are never really alone.

I've learned that even the loyal friends or loved ones who stand by, watch, and care for you may feel this loneliness. Most likely they have never been on this journey either and, if given the choice, certainly wouldn't be walking it now. They wonder what to do and the right time to do it. The questions race in their minds: what to say, when to say it, and what not to say. They want desperately to help but are unable to offer any real help—the kind that will take the disease away. Your loved ones have secret fears—living without a spouse, raising the children alone, concern for finances among other things. These cannot be shared without running the risk of laying guilt, seeming insensitive, or appearing to fish for pity. For the loved ones and friends too, there's a certain and definite loneliness.

Being alone and lonely *is* a dreadful thing. Yet even in this, the people of God are blessed like no other and can actually boast that they are never really alone. You see, others may leave but not the Lord. Others may forget or withdraw but not the Savior-God. Never. So it was with Paul. He shared the events of his preliminary hearing, "At my first defense, no one came to my support, but everyone deserted me. May it not be held against them. But the Lord stood at my side and gave me strength, so that through me the message might be fully proclaimed and all the Gentiles might hear it. And I was delivered from the lion's mouth" (2 Timothy 4:16,17).

> Others may leave or withdraw or desert us but not this God of ours.

Yes, others may leave or withdraw or desert us but not this God of ours. Never. He sticks closer than a friend and even closer than a spouse. Like Paul, every Christian can be certain of it and boast about it. We have peace and strength because of God's promise and the unchanging truth of his own Word. The Lord has deep affection for us: "In Christ Jesus you are all children of God" (Galatians 3:26). He promises that his waiting ears are always open to our lonely cries: "Trust in him at all times, you people; pour out your hearts to him, for God is our refuge" (Psalm 62:8). He encourages us to approach him in prayer: "Through faith in [Christ] we may approach God with freedom and confidence" (Ephesians 3:12). He assures us that he is our dear Father who "is able to do immeasurably more than all we ask or imagine" (Ephesians 3:20). Even in the weakness, pain, and isolation of cancer, he stands by our side. While others may depart, leaving us lonely, nothing "in all creation, will be able to separate us from the love of God that is in Christ Jesus our Lord" (Romans 8:39). No cancer can shake this God of yours whose love for you is so deep that he offered up his life to cleanse you and make you his own forever. You can boast that such a God is yours.

But there is more for the lonely. Having bound himself to us, the Lord also binds us to a unique family. Through our faith in Jesus, we are also children of God. Others like us live in the peace, joy, and certainty of life forever through Christ alone. We are all family—brothers and sisters with our big brother Jesus. Our hearts have been refashioned and made new by the powerful message of God's saving love. The Holy Spirit has given us new hearts that love our brother Jesus and all our brothers and sisters who love him.

The spiritual bond in this family is so real and the connection in Christ is so deep and intimate that, as with the many and different members of a human body, "if one part suffers, every part suffers with it" (1 Corinthians 12:26). Sympathy, yes, but more than sympathy. Sharing a family member's suffering and weakness leads to meaningful and loving action. It comes from love for a brother or sister in Christ who is in need of compassion, kindness, and comfort, especially in his or her pain and misery. God has radically changed the hearts and lives of his people by his own selfless, saving, and active love so we love one another.

Even as many withdrew and abandoned Paul during his final imprisonment, the apostle could nevertheless write, "May the Lord show mercy to the household of Onesiphorus, because he often refreshed me and was not ashamed of my chains. On the contrary, when he was in Rome, he searched hard for me until he found me" (2 Timothy 1:16,17). That man with the strange name is a noble example of one whose heart had been transformed by the love of Christ and went out of his way to actively demonstrate love for his brother. Others also appeared during the apostle's last days, just as they had throughout his ministry. Brothers and sisters—family members in Christ—supported Paul in his mission work; offered financial assistance and prayers; and provided personal company, food, and lodging. They answered Paul's pleas for help and, above all, comfort—comfort that was theirs in the promises of the gospel of Christ and theirs to share with their weak and lonely brother.

For more than two centuries, Christians have been singing a hymn praising God for the unique gift of this special family:

> Blest be the tie that binds our hearts in Christian love;
> the fellowship of kindred minds is like to that above.

> Before our Father's throne we pour our ardent prayers;
> our fears, our hopes, our aims are one, our comforts
>   and our cares.

> We share our mutual woes, our mutual burdens bear,
> and often for each other flows the sympathizing
>   tear. (CW 730:1-3)

When you belong to Christ, you belong to this family—*his* family. Your sisters and brothers will help you bear your burdens no matter what your sorrow is. God has brought you into his family of believers, especially for times like this, so that they might be the channels of his love—brothers and sisters who are ready to support you, help you bear your burdens, pray with you, and tell you again and again what you really need to hear. They will remind you that you have a Savior who will never desert you. Their hearts, after all, are also beating with the love of Christ and a love for you.

> When you belong to Christ, you belong to this family—*his* family.

Although it may be awkward to do so, sometimes you may have to ask for help. But it's all right to ask these people. In fact, they want you to ask because sometimes they don't know how to help you or if you want the help. Yet they often want to help you carry your load. They may drive you to the doctor when you're too weak. They can visit with you, watch your kids, pick up your groceries, prepare your meals, or clean your home. They want to give you an open and sympathetic ear when you just need to vent. They can be there if you need someone to sit quietly and supportively at your side. Of course, they want to offer their powerful prayers for you, read from the Bible with you, and remind you of God's unbreakable promises. Many of them *want* to do these things. Ask. Don't be afraid. Don't deprive your brothers and sisters of the opportunity to help you.

The apostle Paul knew the rich blessings of being inseparably bound to this family and especially to the Father of this family through his Son the Savior. Paul leaned on this family for support in his final days. His brothers and sisters in Christ were concerned for him. He was also filled with love and concern for them. He felt it was important to share the comfort about the future he had as a brother in Christ. In his letter to Timothy, he wrote freely and pointedly about what he would face. He also shared

> He also shared his thoughts about his death. . . . He shared the comfort all believers have in their Savior Jesus.

his thoughts about his death. Perhaps that subject is difficult or off-limits to you or your friends in Christ. Yet Paul could write about death. *His* death. He could write about it freely and openly because he had a view of death that was out of step with the world around him. Paul wanted to comfort the believers and strengthen them after he was gone, so he wrote about his death. He shared the comfort all believers have in their Savior Jesus.

These are among the very last words that we have from the pen of the faithful apostle: "I am already being poured out like a drink offering, and the time for my departure is near. I have fought the good fight, I have finished the race, I have kept the faith. Now there is in store for me the crown of righteousness, which the Lord, the righteous Judge, will award to me on that day—and not only to me, but also to all who have longed for his appearing" (2 Timothy 4:6-8).

Apparently, the wheels were already in motion to bring about Paul's death. He describes it as being poured out completely like the drink offering of wine in the Old Testament. But he was not terrified or overcome with grief at the prospect of dying as a martyr. By God's gracious power, Paul remained steadfast in his faith in Christ Jesus as his Savior. Trusting in Christ alone, Paul was confident that upon his death, as horrible or painful as it might be, he would receive "the crown of righteousness" (2 Timothy 4:8). He wrote from prison. His crown of righteousness would be completely different from what he experienced in chains as a criminal. The Romans thought they would be rid of him. The hope Paul had was an absolute mystery to so many. Upon his death, he would receive a crown and an eternal life lived in perfection, righteousness, and complete innocence and blessedness.

Paul's confidence was rock-solid. A few lines later he wrote, "The Lord will rescue me from every evil attack and will bring me safely to his heavenly kingdom" (2 Timothy 4:18). Whatever Paul would endure and by whatever means the Romans would inflict, he would not—he *could* not—be destroyed. By faith, he belonged to the Lord Jesus, and the Lord Jesus belonged to him. Paul trusted in the promises that the Lord Jesus, through death, would deliver him to life in heaven.

It is the most intriguing thought to human hearts and minds of every age: life after death. Since the beginning, answers offered by humans give many different options. They often leave people feeling empty, disappointed, and even terrified. We object, "I don't want to go out of existence." Others comment, "I don't want to come back in a different form that will be determined by how well I'm living this present life" or "I don't want to come back as a cricket . . . or worse." One suggestion is that we simply live on in the hearts, minds, and memories of others. But one might say, "That's not life. That's death. I want more." The more is the life Paul wrote about that made him so confident. It is real life—a physical, eternal life with a crown. This answer is not one that comes from human thought or speculation. It comes from the One who overcame death and rose from his grave. It is tied to Jesus Christ.

Let Paul speak to you again (something he wrote to the congregation in Corinth):

> What I received I passed on to you as of first importance: that Christ died for our sins according to the Scriptures, that he was buried, that he was raised on the third day according to the Scriptures, and that he appeared to [Peter], and then to the Twelve. After that, he appeared to more than five hundred of the brothers and sisters at the same time, most of whom are still living, though some have fallen asleep. Then he appeared to James, then to all the apostles, and last of all he appeared to me also. (1 Corinthians 15:3-8)

If a real and physical life in that glorious and heavenly kingdom is tied to Jesus Christ, then it is a certainty. Christ himself "was raised" (1 Corinthians 15:4)! He truly came back to life after being truly dead. Check the record on both. Listen to the hundreds of eyewitnesses to both. Jesus was truly dead. In fact, he had to die. As the holy Son of God, he allowed the guilt and sin of the entire world to be placed on his unblemished record. Although he was innocent, he became the world's substitute.

> If a real and physical life in that glorious and heavenly kingdom is tied to Jesus Christ, then it is a certainty.

The just and almighty God has solemnly declared that sinners must die. So on the cross of Calvary, Jesus paid that price in full, suffering the consequences of every person's sins. God had provided the perfect sacrifice for humanity's sin. Because Jesus suffered for our sins, through faith in him we are free of sin's penalty. Sin is forgiven and paid for through the only sacrifice and death that could accomplish it: that of the Son of God himself.

Did he actually do that? Yes, "he was raised on the third day" (1 Corinthians 15:4). Sin is forgiven, and Jesus promised, "God so loved the world that he gave his one and only Son, that whoever believes in him shall not perish but have eternal life" (John 3:16).

Even as Paul sat alone in his darkened cell, chained like a criminal and viewing his impending death, he wrote ecstatically to Timothy that "Christ Jesus . . . has destroyed death and has brought life and immortality to light through the gospel" (2 Timothy 1:10).

It may seem just like human dreams and the opinions of others. We base our hope for that life to come on God's promises and the resurrection of Jesus. But we must wait for it. Unless Jesus returns first, our weak and frail bodies will enter a grave. Relying on Jesus and his promises, we believe that death and the grave have already been rendered powerless over us by Jesus. Neither can hold us. Paul explained it to the Corinthians: "For as in Adam all die, so in Christ all will be made alive. But each in turn: Christ, the firstfruits; then, when he comes, those who belong to him" (1 Corinthians 15:22,23). We too, like our Savior, will come out of our graves. And we too will live forever. We have to because sin has been removed; death and the grave have no power over us any longer.

Now for you with cancer. You are so weak and so wearied by it. Consider what the hope that Jesus promises means to you. The bodies with which we'll come out of the grave will be entirely different than the body that goes into the grave. Paul explained what it meant, "The body that is sown is perishable" (1 Corinthians 15:42). That we know. Every person on the planet, whether he or she wants to deal with this fact, knows deep down that it is still fact. We die and are buried. But God promises that's not the end. For those in Christ, the same body that dies "is raised imperishable." Our imperishable bodies rise, never to decay. They will never die again—in fact, they are incapable.

In addition, our present bodies are "sown in dishonor" (1 Corinthians 15:43). Dishonor? We try to respect the dead by dressing the body in fine clothing, placing it in an expensive casket, and surrounding the casket with sprays of flowers. But it is also true that at the end of the funeral service we place the decomposing corpse in a hole and cover it with dirt. There's nothing honorable about that. Yet in Christ, that very same body will be "raised in glory" with a beauty and radiance—nothing at all to shrink away from or hide from sight. Your present body, especially in your declining years, "is sown in weakness." Even now, regardless of your age—you with cancer know this well, don't you? But understand this: for those in Christ, the very same weak, wearied, diseased, and worn-out body "is raised in power" (1 Corinthians 15:43). No disease. No cancer. No nausea. No chemo, radiation, surgery, or pain. But victory! Your body will be perfect beyond anything you have ever known or can imagine. Perfect forever.

> For those in Christ, the very same weak, wearied, diseased, and worn-out body "is raised in power."

A while back, on a particularly bad and sad day for Linda, she told me that it is especially at those times that she welcomes death. I understood. I was not offended that she was ready to leave me, her children and grandchildren, and a life in which the Lord had so richly blessed both of us. After all, he has prepared something incomparably greater for both of us. And it is certain. The "crown of righteousness" (2 Timothy 4:8), no more sin in or around us, no more sorrow. The weakness, CLL, cancer, pain, and tears will be gone. Because of Jesus, she looked forward to nothing but the glory everlasting, the perfect and eternal union with Christ, and a happy reunion with our loved ones in Christ. How could she not welcome that?

It's yours too. In Christ, it is yours. You must wait for it to come. I know that's difficult. But wait we all must. Our prayers for a cure and return to normal life may be answered. Whatever the Lord sends—more life here or in heaven—he asks us to wait. Will you wait? Can you? Just a little longer now. You swear you can't wait any longer, but you can. He is with you—this God of yours— with a love you never thought existed and with strong arms into which you can collapse. He's there with promises that nothing can possibly change, filling you with a hope that is certain—a glorious future and life beyond this one. Will you wait? Just a little longer. It's coming. Then it will be a hope *realized!* His promise sustains you and all Christians while we are waiting here. You long for a body changed in the twinkling of an eye, better than springing out of bed again. You will spring to life again in perfect wholeness and strength. Then you will serve the Savior whom you will finally see face-to-face. Victory! Unending victory! Eternal victory! Will you wait? Please do. Wait with me. Wait with Linda. Let's do it together. While we wait, let's do a little boasting: "When I am weak, even then I am so strong in Christ—in Christ alone." That's your boast in life, death, and life unending. Christ alone.

> Will you wait? Just a little longer. It's coming. Then it will be a hope *realized!* His promise sustains you and all Christians while we are waiting here.

Grace be with you.